D1233106

THE LAST SHEAF

THE LAST SHEAF

Essays by

EDWARD THOMAS

With a Foreword by

THOMAS SECCOMBE

Essay Index Reprint Series

BOOKS FOR LIBRARIES PRESS
FREEPORT, NEW YORK

First Published 1928
Reprinted 1972

Library of Congress Cataloging in Publication Data

Thomas, Edward, 1878-1917.
    The last sheaf; essays.

    (Essay index reprint series)
    Reprint of the 1928 ed.
    I. Title.
PR6039.H55L4 1972   824'.9'12   73-167427
ISBN 0-8369-2673-0

PRINTED IN THE UNITED STATES OF AMERICA
BY
NEW WORLD BOOK MANUFACTURING CO., INC.
HALLANDALE, FLORIDA 33009

CONTENTS

FOREWORD

I HAVE seldom received a fiercer shock than when, from a few lines of appreciation, as beautiful as sympathetic, in this morning's Roll of Honour in *The Times*, I learned that Edward Thomas had given his life in this war. It was the life of one who knew and loved England, its inhabitants and its writers, old and new, better than any man I ever came across.

About twelve years ago he denied with much embarrassment the imputation of writing an extremely critical review (in the *Academy*, I think it was) of a Literary History for which I was mainly responsible. Very few living men had the knowledge *plus* the insight to have written that review. He *may* have been guiltless, but at any rate the incident marks the beginning of a friendship. Thomas had what are vaguely called 'Celtic' characteristics; he was, as his name betokens, Welsh, and he sorrowed at times over the loss of his birthright in the Cambrian tongue. He knew Wales and its taverns intimately from the Worm's Head to Penmaenmawr (I met him once in the Gower Inn and once at the summit of Cereg Cennyn Castle); *Wild Wales* he savoured intensely, and I expect he knew nearly as much Welsh as Borrow. It would have been easy to say that he adored *Lavengro* and *Wild Wales*, but, as a matter of fact, there were few books that he praised unreservedly – Milton, Browne, Cobbett, W. H. Hudson, and the Gissing who wrote *By the Ionian Sea*, were among those to whom he recurred most freely. His knowledge of poetry soon took me out of my depth. To the younger men he was a Rhadamanthus and a Cerberus in one. He was the man with the keys to the Paradise of English Poetry, and probably reviewed more modern verse than any critic of his time. The material bulk of it became in the lapse of years a source of vexation to him. He was debarred from bestowing his presentation copies as Lamb did – over the garden wall amid a neighbour's cabbages. The price of the paper for pulping was exceeded by the cost of cartage. Burning and burying were altogether too expensive. The demands of a neighbouring school for kitetails and paper chases made hardly any impression. He acquired the habit of taking the books about with him in a heavy valise and leaving them, as it were accidentally, at the houses of friends. Of these he had many, even among poets; and some of them I know, such as W. H. Davies, W. de la Mare, and J. Freeman, would regard him as a counsellor unrivalled.

Poetic as he was in appearance and fortune,

FOREWORD

Thomas was fundamentally a humorist; and nothing was more delightful than to hear him expatiate on the latent humour (perceptible to him alone, in a measure) of a friend – such as Edward Garnett, for instance. His misfortune as an author was that he began too early. At eighteen he was a formed writer. It amused him to study history at Lincoln, under Owen Edwards, but even then he was contributing finished verse and prose to the literary weeklies. He formed himself on the school of White, Jefferies, Burroughs, and Hudson, and perhaps surpassed them all in sheer technique. His Reisebilder and his Prose Eclogues of the Southern England that he specially loved could hardly be matched. The quality of his prose was apt to be too costly for the modern market; and the result was often Love and Literature, with its precarious awards, literally in a cottage. There is such a thing as Welsh influence, no doubt; but there is also a Welsh pride, and Thomas would be beholden to no man for a penny that he had not earned. His pride in the dignity of letters was intense. The result was much hard and sometimes unsympathetic collar work mostly of a biographical complexion, the best of which (and in his *Jefferies* and his *Borrow* it is very good indeed) shows marks of fatigue. His system of writing was almost too

9

intensive, if that be possible. He rose early, performed certain domestic duties (for a servant was rare in his household), and then walked a mile or more uphill in his Hampshire home, to a small, solitary summer-house – not unlike George Borrow's at Oulton. There he composed in absolute isolation those stories and scenes of country life and the English atmosphere of things in which he has had few rivals and no superiors. He was a desperate student of the *genre* that he adopted, and his anthology *This England* – the best, I think, ever done – is really an artist's notebook. It annotates the life-enthusiasm of a born prosemaster, whose love of this country was as generous as it was instinctive. I wished, he says, 'to make a book as full of English character and country as an egg is of meat. If I have reminded others, as I did myself continually, of some of the echoes called up by the name of England, I am satisfied.'

The praise of what we love is sweeter when we are beginning to fear that we may lose it, as we began to fear in that summer-like autumn of 1914. Newman's home-truths, followed by his 'I'd rather be an Englishman (as, in fact, I am) than belong to any other race under heaven,' or Lord Mansfield's 'The air of England has long been too pure for a slave, and every man is free who breathes it,' stir us more, and more deeply, than the explicit apostrophe of the professed patriot. This Thomas perceived. The sincerity of his own feeling he expressed not in words, but in deeds. Noble in appearance, with some of the best traits of Christopher North, though he seldom spoke enthusiastically save of his friends and the idols of his youth (Swinburne, Meredith, Hardy), and of the countryside and its figures, indefatigable on foot or awheel, a complete connoisseur of the inns of Southland, ardent in friendship and hospitality, in spite of his deep temperamental melancholy, touching at times almost upon hypochondria, his loss is a knockdown blow. Three years ago he was a typical Liberal of the Intelligentsia. But he was quick to recognize the chink in the armour of the pacifist philosophy. He saw that the one remedy was victory, and he dedicated himself, a humble unit, to attain that. The event electrified some of his friends. They said, 'This man was a born soldier.'

THOMAS SECCOMBE

GLENCAIRN, CAMBERLEY,
April 16, 1917.

*⁎*This note was originally printed in the form of a letter addressed to the Editor of *The Times Literary Supplement.*

THE LAST SHEAF

HOW I BEGAN

Talking prose is natural to most of the species; writing it is now almost as common, if not as natural; having it published when written is the third step which distinguishes an author from the more primitive minority of mankind. No author, I suppose, except Miss Helen Keller, has varied this method of progress. Every one begins by talking, stumbles into writing, and succumbs to print.

The first step is the most interesting and the most difficult to explain and describe. I shall leave it alone. The second step is very interesting, and less difficult to explain and describe, yet I can remember little of it. I can only remark here that the result of teaching a child to read before it can write is that it begins and usually ends by writing like a book, not like a human being. It was my own experience. From the age of one, I could express by words and inflections of the voice all that ever sought expression within me, from feelings of heat, cold, hunger, repletion, indigestion, etc., to subtle preferences of persons and things. But when I came to write the slowness of that unnatural act decimated and disconcerted my natural faculties. I laboriously covered a square foot of notepaper, communicating nothing much beyond the fact that I had begun to hold a pen, and to master English grammar.

That the best of fountain-pens is slow, does not entirely account for the inexpressiveness of that square foot of notepaper. The slowness made it practically impossible to say what I was thinking, even if I had tried. I did not try hard. I do not believe that it was by any means my sole or chief aim to write what I was thinking, or what I should have spoken had my correspondent been in the same room with me. I felt it to be highly important that I should use terms such as I had met in books, seldom if ever in speech. Nor do I remember hearing it said that I could, or should, write as I thought or as I spoke.

Until the age of eight or nine, therefore, all my writing was painful and compulsory, and I knew well that it displayed a poorer creature than the severest critic could judge me. But at that age I was given a small notebook in a cover as much like tortoiseshell as could be made for a penny. In this I wrote down a number of observations of my own accord, though I dare say the notebook had been designed as a trap; if there was a separate bait, I have forgotten it. All that I can remember is that I pronounced the houses of Swindon to be 'like bull-dogs, small but strongly built.' They were of stone, and I was accustomed to brick. Stone seemed to be a grander material. Hence the note. The sentennious form was, no doubt, due to a conscious desire to be impressive, that is to say, adult. It was not the last time I experienced this desire, but I shall not trouble you with more instances.

With short intervals, from that time onwards I was a writer by choice. I began several diaries, carrying on the entries in some of them as far as February. By the time I was fourteen or fifteen, I did more; I kept a more or less daily record of notable events, the finding of birds' nests, the catching of moles or fish, the skinning of a stoat, the reading of Richard Jefferies and the naturalists.

These notes aimed at brevity: they were above syntax and indifferent to dignity. I was not, however, permitted to forget syntax or dignity. I was obliged to write essays on Imperial Federation, the Greek Colonization of Sicily, Holidays, etc., where I gave myself up to an almost purely artistic rendering of such facts as I remembered, and such opinions as I could concoct by the help of memory, fancy, and the radical and the free-thinking influence of home. Thus, like nearly every other child, I virtually neglected in my writing the feelings that belonged to my own nature and my own times of life – an irreparable loss, whether great or not. If I wrote about what really pleased or concerned me, like a walk all day or all night in Wiltshire, I had in view not the truth but the eyes of elders, and those elders clothed in the excess and circumstance of elderliness regularly assumed in the presence of children. I was considered to excel in this form of rhetoric. So seriously, too, did I take myself in it, that from the time I was sixteen I found myself hardly letting a week pass without writing one or two descriptions – of a man, or a place, or a walk – in a manner largely founded on Jefferies' *Amateur Poacher*, Kingsley's *Prose Idylls*, and Mr. Francis A. Knight's weekly contributions to the *Daily News*, but doubtless with tones supplied also by Shelley and Keats, and later on by Ruskin, De Quincey, Pater, and Sir Thomas Browne. I had quite a number of temptations to print, and at the age of fifteen easily gave way. At seventeen, some of those descriptions were printed in the *Speaker* and the *New Age*, and soon afterwards took the form of a book.

While I was afflicted with serious English composition and English literature, I was reading Scott, Fenimore Cooper, Henty, and the travellers, because I loved them; I was also thinking and talking in a manner which owed little to those dignified exercises, though the day was to come when I spoke very much as I wrote. Presently, also, myself and English, as she is taught in schools, came to a conflict, and gradually to a more and more friendly agreement through the necessity of writing long letters daily to one who was neither a schoolboy nor an elder, the subject of the letters being matters concerning nobody else in the world. Now it was that I had a chance of discarding or of adapting to my own purpose the fine words and infinite variety of constructions which I had formerly admired from afar off and imitated in fairly cold blood. There is no doubt that my masters often lent me dignity and subtlety altogether beyond my needs.

Both in these letters and in papers intended for print, I ravaged the language (to the best of my ability) at least as much for ostentation as for use, though I should not like to have to separate the two. This must always happen where a man has collected all the colours of the rainbow, 'of earthquake and eclipse,' on his palette, and has a cottage or a gasometer to paint. A continual negotiation was going on between thought, speech and writing, thought having as a rule the worst of it. Speech was humble and creeping, but wanted too many fine shades and could never come to a satisfactory end. Writing was lordly and regardless. Thought went on in the twilight, and wished the other two might come to terms for ever. But maybe they did not and never will, and, perhaps, they never do. In my own case, at any rate, I cannot pronounce, though I have by this time provided an abundance of material for a judgment.

MIDSUMMER

THE gold lilies have unclosed on Haweswater, and the wind does not raise the green discs of leaf: the sedge-warblers chatter and sing all day on the sedges above the silver shallows. It is midsummer.

Next to being with spring when it comes to the moors and mountains is being with midsummer. When spring comes it is often, as it were, a lamb snatched from the teeth of winter. It is pale and trembling, a shade overhangs it; it is doubtful, mysterious, and one has need of faith to believe that it will grow up and become strong and bold. But now, with midsummer, it is impossible to suppose that winter can overcome it. And especially in this year of years. There have been no springs like it. The others have led up to this, which must break away from all precedents.

Day after day the wind blows from the south, usually a rainy quarter here, yet no rain falls. Thunder skirts us, an impotent barbaric decoration, a lion that roars like a dove in the gossamer haze veiling Helvellyn northward. Nothing invades this charmed fortress between sea and mountains. A magic circle protects it. It seems to be midsummer itself, an island in the midst of summer, close to the shore of spring, out of sight of autumn. For if it be reasonable as well as customary to call this solstice midsummer, it is because the year leaps forward rapidly up to this point, and then declines – or used to do in the old years – very slowly from the summit. If examined it might prove as transitory as any of the moments of spring. The thunder that hovers circling round us might burst in to-night. But some of the marks of change are less obvious now than in spring. The greens of the leaves are mature, yet will last some time. The fading of blossoms has by midsummer become familiar, and we notice it less than when primroses are being torn, bluebells drying up, may browning and dropping. The succession of flowers has been so continuous that it promises to have no end. The year has outgrown some of the beautiful refinements and perturbations of spring, like the interchanging and overlapping melancholy and excitement of youth.

I have called this a charmed fortress. But it is no garden elaborately guarded and secluded. No. Chinese wall has been built to keep out autumn and winter. On the contrary, childlike boldness has placed it where they could never suspect their victim of being so guileless as to hide. It is on a high, open hill-top among rocks and stunted trees, through which I see hills scarred or wooded a mile or two distant, and mountains that might be clouds on the horizon. There is no garden, simply because the rabbits have not been shot. Wild roses, both white and, with butter-coloured hearts, overtop the stone walls in places; otherwise, the noticeable flower is the coral of the Scots firs among young shoots like silver candles. No, it is not a garden; it is but a ground where the sun can dwell all the long day and bank his heat in grass and short bracken and stones. Flowers there are – rock roses of thin yellow silk, and white lady's bedstraw, and thyme – but the bird's-eye primroses, rose-purple clusters smelling like primroses by the waterside, the violet meadow-cranesbills among the dusty nettle and parsley of the roadside, cannot climb here. Higher up, the rock rose fails, and only herb Robert thrusts up a flower among crumbs of stone. There, even some of the grass has withered to a skeleton, and the mosses that were like moles of gilt olive have parched and darkened. Half the hill limestone, now high boulders, now smoothly corrugated pavements, now flakes vertically rotted, now crumbled scree, now flat plates that ring like crockery or like iron. (Years ago someone collected plates of this stone that rang through a whole scale of music.) Sometimes a juniper has penetrated the stones and spread foliage of palest and blackest green out over them in a bush like an umbrella with no handle. But of the junipers the dead are more numerous than the living.

Often I hear no music but the stones ringing as I walk, unless a peewit cries, or a wheatear, flitting about me, says alternately 'chuck' and 'sweet.' Once or twice in the day, far away over the pallid rock and misted dark bushes, a cuckoo calls; not the cuckoo of the South Country, to whom the poet has been repeating for several weeks the line:

'Tune thy two strings and break the third.'

but a faultless cuckoo. I have not once seen him. He is as vague as Helvellyn northward, or Ingleborough eastward. His note seems an echo, long treasured, and now delivered up by the rocks of Whitbarrow, that make two arched leaps and then fall perpendicularly to the flat river land. His voice skirts us; being a perishing thing it does not really enter the circle.

But the nightjar is the bird of midsummer. At nightfall he perches on the tip of a Scots fir's topmost silver candle and reels his churr. The hum of insects is to midsummer heat what the kettle's singing is to water beginning to boil. The nightjar's 'purr' represents the water seething, bubbling, and lifting the lid. The wind has gone up into Scotland. The air is still. The nightjar fills the broad night with a noise as of a shadowy brook running over the dry, pale rocks of the hills. While he sings, taking breath at moments, he looks from side to side on his perch, then suddenly ends, and slips off silently. His next perch is distant, and I can hear him only if I listen for him. Again he shifts, this time out of hearing. For a time there is no sound on earth, only an owl that cries like a huntsman among the mountains of the moon, winding his horn.

CHALK PITS

I is sometimes consoling to remember how
  much of the pleasantness of English country is
due to men, by chance or design. The sowing of
various crops, the planting of hedges and building
of walls, the trimming of woods to allow trees to
grow large and shapely, and so on, are among the
designed causes of this pleasantness. Here men
have obviously co-operated with Nature. But as
great effects are produced when they have seemed
at first to insult or ignore her. A new house, for
example, however well proportioned, and however
wisely chosen the material, is always harsh to the
eye and the mind. In a hundred years it little
matters what the form or the material; if the house
survives, and is inhabited for a century, it has
probably made its place. If it is deserted, it makes
a place yet more rapidly. There is no building
which the country cannot digest and assimilate if
left to itself in about twenty years. Cottage or
factory or mansion is powerless against frost, wind,
rain, grass and ivy, and the entirely assimilated
building is always attractive unless the beholder
happens to know the reason why it was deserted;
and even if he does, his sympathy will very likely
not conflict with his sense of beauty, but will aid
it in secret – that is what is consoling. London

27

deserted would become a much pleasanter place than Richard Jefferies pictured it in *After London*. The mere thought of the jackdaws who would dwell there is a cheerful one, and they would not be alone. I like to think what mysteries the shafts, the tubes, the tunnels and the vaults would make, and what a place to explore. The railway cuttings, unless very steep-sided, soon become romantic, and near London they are a refuge for many plants and insects.

But among the works of men that rapidly become works of Nature, and can be admired without misanthropy, are the chalk and marl pits. The great ones are pleasing many miles away, both in themselves and through association. On a hill-side they always assume a good shape, like those of a scallop shell or even of a fan. Those on the Downs above Lewes, Maidstone and Midhurst, will be remembered. Against their white walls we can like the limeworks themselves, whether they offer only the ordinary black chimneys as at Buriton, or whether they are majestic in their arched masonry like those which are consuming the Dinas above Llandebie in Carmarthenshire. If there were only one of these fans or scallops of white low down on a bare hill-side it would be as celebrated as the inverted fan of Fujiyama in Japan. They are impressive, I think, chiefly as being, with the exception of glass-houses and sheets of water, the only distinctly luminous objects on the comparatively dark earth. They show up like arched windows or doorways of gigantic proportions lighted from within the hills. Their all but perpendicular walls take long to be grassed over when deserted, even if the rabbits do not seek refuge in them and keep the chalk moving by their narrow terraces. Perhaps that enormous scoop is one that has been so grassed over, on the steep hill-side facing southward near East Meon. It is completely covered with fine grass, and has an almost level green floor, which is used as a playing field. It bears the name of 'The Vineyard,' and it has been suggested that it was used by the Romans or Romanized Britons for the cultivation of vines. But this is very much like one of the lesser natural coombes of the chalk country, and except for its name, and possible use, it has no particular interest. The lesser chalk pits are the better. These may be divided roughly into two kinds – first, those which are dug out of more or less level ground, and are shaped like a bowl or funnel, or a series of such; second, those which have been carved out of a slope. Those upon a slope are usually the more charming to the eye. They are met, for example, suddenly where the road bends round a steep bank, and whether the chalk is dazzling or shadowed it is welcome. The white or grey-white wall is over-hung by roots of ash and beech trees, and if it be old by a curtain of traveller's joy or ivy. These overhanging roots and climbers often form a covered way large enough for a man to creep through, and much used by foxes and lesser beasts. At the foot is a waste space of turf. Here grows the wayfaring tree with its pendent clusters of cherry-coloured fruit, or the beam tree, whose leaves fall with their heavy sides uppermost and so lie all through the winter; or perhaps bracken and purple-stemmed angelica, nine feet high and straight, with graceful bracketed frondage all still; or perhaps the sweetest flowers of the chalk, the yellow St. John's wort, birdsfoot, agrimony, and hawkweed, the pink bramble and mallow, the mauve marjoram and basil, the purple knapweed, and to these come the Red Admiral and Peacock and Copper butterflies, the bright-winged flies and bees, and the grasshoppers like emerald armoured horsemen – four white butterflies float past hundreds of flowers without heeding them, and then all four try to alight on one. The air is full of the sweetness of wild carrot and parsnip seeds. Some-times the floor is filled up with a dense Paradise of bramble and blackthorn, and there is a night-ingale in it or a blackcap and in the winter a wren.

The hollow pits are not so familiar, because they lie often in the middle of the fields which they used to supply with chalk. They may be so shallow that they have been ploughed over, and now merely serve to break the surface of a great corn-field. Or they may be deep like mines, so that the chalk had to be raised by a windlass; and these are now protected by rails, and used only for depositing carrion. As a rule the bowl-shaped pits have been overgrown by bushes, or where large enough, planted with trees, with beech, oak, ash and holly; and they are surrounded by a hedge to keep out cattle. They have names of their own; often they are dells, such as Stubridge Dell, or Slade Dell. Thus they often form pretty little islands of copse in the midst of arable, and show their myriads of primroses or bluebells through the hazels when the neighbour field is crumbling dry in an east wind. These islands are attractive largely, I think, because they suggest fragments of primæval forest that have been left untouched by the plough on account of their roughness. I call them islands because that is the impression made on the passer-by. Cross over to them, and they are seen to be more like ponds full of everything but water. There are some small ones brimful of purple rosebay flowers in the midst of the corn. Others are full of all that a goldfinch loves – teasel, musk, thistle and sunshine. One is so broken up by the uneven diggings, the roots of trees, and the riot of brambles that a badger is safe in it with a whole pack of children. Some farms have one little or big dell to almost every field, and to enter-prising children there must be large tracts of country which exist chiefly to provide these dells. One or two of the best of them are half-way between the hollow pit and the hill-side scoop. One in particular, a vast one, lies under a steep road which bends round it, and has to protect its passengers by posts and rails above the perpendicular. At the upper side it is precipitous, but it has a level floor, and the old entrance below is by a very gradual descent. It is very old, and some of the trees, which are now only butts, must have been two centuries old when they were felled. It is big enough for the Romany Rye to have fought there with the Flaming Tinman. But in Borrow's days it had more trees in it. Now it has about a score of tall ash trees only, ivy covered, and almost branchless, rising up out of it above the level of the road. Except at midsummer, only the tops of

the ash trees catch the sunlight. The rest is dark
and wild, and somehow cruel. The woodmen
looked tiny and dark, as if working for a punishment, when they were felling some of the trees
below. That hundred yards or so of road running
round the edge of the ancient pit is as fascinating
as any other similar length in England. From the
rails above you could well watch the Romany Rye
and the Flaming Tinman and fair-haired Isopel.
But except the woodmen and the horses drawing
out the timber, no one visits it. It is too gloomy.
This is no vineyard, unless for growing the ruby
grape of Proserpine, the nightshade. Though
roofed with the sky, it has the effect of a cave, an
entrance to the underworld.

Other roadside dells, facing the south or south-
west, are not so deserted. The old chalk pits, being
too steep and rough to be cultivated, soon grow
into places as wild as ancient Britain. They are
especially good at a meeting of several roads.
They form wayside wastes which are least easily
enclosed. These strips are, or were, called slangs,
and a waste of a larger kind gave us the curious
word Flash. Flash is a village in a wild quarter of
Derbyshire, between Buxton and Macclesfield.
The people were mostly squatters who used the
place as headquarters when they were not travel-

ling to and from the fairs; and the lingo in which
they talked to one another was called flash-talk.
There is flash-talk still to be heard in some of the
wayside chalk pits. There is no better place for a
camp than one of these with a good aspect. It
gives a man a little of the sense of a room. At the
best it has almost four walls, which keep out
neither sun nor rain. Some of them are much
used by tramps and gipsies and other travellers,
until they are enclosed on the ground that these
persons are a nuisance or are spoiling the beauty
of the country. I think these travellers ought to be
protected – say by the Zoological Society. Many
of them are happy and they are at least as interesting, though often not as beautiful, as anything
at the Zoo. They cost very little, being far too
meek to steal much. For the price of a first-rate
cigar one of them could be fed for a week, or a
family for a bottle of wine. They give endless
quiet amusement to civilized men who here behold what they have come from and what some
of them would like to return to again. It seems to
require some philosophy to sit high on the Downs
on a rainy February day, reading half a sheet of a
week-old daily paper, on the leeside of a copse
which was once a chalk pit. I have seen the man
several times, but never observed that anyone was

sitting at his feet to learn his wisdom. He had not wife, nor other possessions, nor desire to converse. He was lean, dirty, quite unpicturesque and not strong, but he made the best of a wet February day. Most men would have preferred to be one of the chestnut horses ploughing near, their coats marked as with the hammer-marks on copper.

In summer, he and his kind are more picturesque. The best group I ever saw – and it was at the entrance to a chalk pit – was three wild women in black rags, with a perambulator and a large black cat. They had hair like hemp, and glittering blue eyes. They were lean but tall and strong. They were quite silent. When I first saw them they had a fire and were cooking – the cat knew what – upon a windy Sunday morning, while the church bells were ringing.

They were not supernatural, I can swear, because one of them asked the time as I left, though it was upon a solitary and remote roadway, and they appeared to have no affairs in this world that could depend upon 'the time.' I laughed at the question, and they seemed surprised, but they were too busy – thinking, shall I say? – to say any more. Two days later the races at — began, but they were not there. On the morning of the races human beings crawled out of all kinds of holes, and the chalk pits supplied one or two. There is, presumably, no horse-racing after death, so that the lot of these devotees is not to be envied, though in this world they seem content. I saw one crawl out of an archway where a considerable stream of water ran in winter. But the chalk pit was better – it seemed to hold, as in a treasury, half the sun of a glorious morning, and across the floor, beside a dead fire, sprawled a middle-aged sportswoman in old black velvet, fast asleep, though the race-goers were streaming past in some haste. Those were the days of the green-finches – little bands flitting and twittering through hedges and over yew trees with clear thin notes, breezy in the breeze – and of linnets scattering now over the brassy ragwort flowers, and millions of poppies in the wheat. Once I met a small bear in one of the tangled dells in this neighbourhood. He was curled up in the sun between bushes of gorse, and his master's head was buried in his fur. If the bear had been alone it might have been a scene in Britain before Cæsar's time, but though it was 1904 the bear looked indigenous. This dell is one of those which may be natural or artificial, or perhaps partly both, a small natural coombe having been convenient for excavation in the chalk. It lies at the foot of a wild Down which is climbed, chiefly for the sake of its chalk pits, by a slanting steep road. The dell is a long narrow chamber with a floor rising towards the beginning of the steep slope. The sides of it are worn by the rabbits and support little but gaunt elder bushes. The floor grows a few ash trees and much gorse. The tallest tree is dead, but the coombe is sheltered and the great ash still holds up its many arms in the form of a lyre, high above the rest. It is grey and stiff and without bark. But the jackdaws love it. All through the afternoons of summer they come and go among the hills, and the dead tree is their chief station. It might almost seem a religious place to them. There are always two or three perched on the topmost branches, talking to those arriving or departing. Now and then a turtledove flies up and they do not resent it. As to the bear, it was nothing to them. Their ancestors had seen many such. There are jackdaws in the elms of the neighbouring meadows, but those religious ones upon the dead ash tree seem the most important, and it alone is never deserted.

Night after night deliberately we take upon
ourselves the utmost possible weakness, because it is the offering most acceptable to sleep.
Our thick coverings give us warmth without need
of motion. The night air we moderate into a
harmless rustling or stroking coolness; or, if it
be an obstreperous air, we may shut it out altogether, and with it all sounds. We choose to be
alone, and in darkness. We make ourselves so
weak, so easy, so content with nothing, that scarce
anything but personal danger, and that immediate
and certain, could stir us. Thus cunningly we
oppose the utmost possible weakness to the assault
of sleep.

Sometimes I have a lighted candle and a book
at my bedside, but seldom for more than five
minutes. The light and the effort of reading,
though I may have gone early to bed, are too
much for my instinctive weakness, this religious
malingering. I find that I desire to enter without
gradation into perfect helplessness, and I exercise
a quiet resolution against the strains even of
memory. For once I have lain down, safe, warm,
and unanxious, nothing I can remember is worthy
for more than a moment to interrupt. In this
weakness there is a kind of power. Still and re-

39

laxed, as it were lacking bones and muscles entirely, I lie in a composed eagerness for sleep. And most often sleep will stoop and swallow me up, and I have no more dream or trouble than a grain swallowed by a bird.

But the mighty weakness that so allures sleep is turned to a powerless strength during the night. I wake before dawn, and then, much as I desire sleep, I cannot have it. I am now the prey of anything but sleep, anything real or unreal that comes to sight, touch, or hearing, or straight to the brain. It seems that all night I have heard the poplars shivering across the street in the strong lamplight, with a high singing note like a flame instead of a noise of showers; it seems that this shivering and this light will continue for ever, and for ever shall I lie restless under their afflictions. I strive, but no longer with unconscious power, to sink into the weakness that commands or deserves sleep. Any memory now can discompose me; any face, any word, any event, out of the past has to be entertained for a minute or an hour, according to its will, not mine. Those poplar leaves in the bright street are mightier than I or sleep. In vain I seek the posture and simulate the gesture of an already favoured victim. I am too weak. I am too strong, yet I cannot rise and darken the room or go out

and contemn sleep. It is a blessed thing if I am
strong enough at last to wear myself out to sleep.

The other night I awoke just as the robin was
beginning to sing outside in the dark garden.
Beyond him the wind made a moan in the little
fir-copse as of a forest in a space magically enclosed
and silent, and in the intervals of his song silence
fell about him like a cloak which the wind could
not penetrate. As well as I knew the triple cry
farther off for the crow of the first cock, I knew
this for the robin's song, pausing but unbroken,
though it was unlike any song of robin I had heard
in daylight, standing or walking among trees.
Outside, in the dark hush, to me lying prostrate,
patient, unmoving, the song was absolutely monotonous, absolutely expressionless, a chain of little
thin notes linked mechanically in a rhythm identi-
cal at each repetition. This was not the voluntary
personal utterance of a winged sprite that I used
to know, but a note touched on the instrument of
night by a player unknown to me, save that it was
he who delighted in the moaning fir-trees and in
my silence. Nothing intelligible to me was expressed by it; since he, the player, alone knew, I
call it expressionless.

When the light began to arrive, the song in the
enclosed hush, and the sound of the trees beyond

it, remained the same. I remained awake, silently and as stilly as possible, cringing for sleep. I was an unwilling note on the instrument; yet I do not know that the robin was less unwilling. I strove to escape out of that harmony of bird, wind, and man. But as fast as I made my mind a faintly heaving, shapeless, grey blank, some form or colour appeared; memory or anticipation was at work.

Gradually I found myself trying to understand this dawn harmony. I vowed to remember it and ponder it in the light of day. To make sure of remembering I tried putting it into rhyme. I was resolved not to omit the date; and so much so that the first line had to be 'The seventh of September,' nor could I escape from this necessity. Then September was to be rhymed with. The word 'ember' occurred and stayed; no other would respond to all my calling. The third and fourth lines, it seemed, were bound to be something like —

> The sere and the ember
> Of the year and of me.

This gave me no satisfaction, but I was under a very strong compulsion. I could do no more; not a line would add itself to the wretched three; nor did they cease to return again and again to my head. It was fortunate for me as a man, if not as an unborn poet, that I could not forget the lines; for by continual helpless repetition of them I rose yet once more to the weakness that sleep demanded. Gradually I became conscious of nothing but the moan of trees, the monotonous expressionless robin's song, the slightly aching body to which I was, by ties more and more slender, attached. I felt, I knew, I did not think that there would always be an unknown player, always wind and trees, always a robin singing, always a listener listening in the stark dawn: and I knew also that if I were the listener I should not always lie thus in a safe warm bed thinking myself alive. . . . And so I fell asleep again on the seventh of September.

WHEN the five silent travellers saw the colonel coming into their compartment, all but the little girl looked about in alarm to make sure that it was a mere third-class carriage. His expression, which actually meant a doubt, whether it was not perhaps a fourth-class carriage, had deceived them; and one by one -- some with hypocritical, delaying mock-unconsciousness, others with faint meaning looks -- they began to look straight before them again, except while they cast casual eyes on the groups waving or turning away from the departing train. Even then every one looked round suddenly because the colonel knocked the ashes out of his pipe with four sharp strokes on the seat. He himself was looking neither to the right nor to the left. But he was not, therefore, looking up or down or in front of him; he was restraining his eyes from exercise, well knowing that nothing worthy of them was within range. The country outside was ordinary downland, the people beside him were but human beings.

Having knocked out the ashes, he used his eyes. He was admiring the pipe -- without animation, even sternly -- but undoubtedly admiring what he and the nature of things had made of the briar in 1910 and 1911. It had been choice from the beginning, not too big, not too small, neither too long nor too short, neither heavy nor slim; absolutely straight, in no way fanciful, not pretentious; the grain of the wood uniform – a freckled or 'bird's-eye' grain – all over. In his eyes it was faultless, yet not austerely perfect; for it won his affection as well as his admiration by its 'cobby' quality, inclining to be shorter and thicker than the perfect one which he had never yet possessed save in dreams. A woman who by unprompted intelligence saw the merit of this favourite could have done anything with the colonel; but no woman ever did, though when instructed by him they all assented in undiscriminating warmth produced by indifference to the pipe and veneration for its master. As for the men, he had chosen his friends too well for there to be one among them who could not appreciate the beauty of the pipe, the exquisitely trained understanding of the colonel.

He was not merely its purchaser; in fact, it was not yet paid for. The two years of expectant respect, developing into esteem, cordial admiration, complacent satisfaction, had not been a period of indolent possession. Never once had he failed in alert regard for the little briar, never overheated it, never omitted to let it rest when smoked

46

out, never dropped it or left it about among the profane, never put into it any but the tobacco which now, after many years, he thought the best, the only, mixture. Its dark chestnut with an amber overgleam was reward enough.

As he filled the pipe he allowed his eyes to alight on it with a kindliness well on this side of discretion, yet unmistakable once the narrow but subtle range of his emotional displays had been gauged. He showed no haste as he kept his pale, short second finger working by a fine blend of instinct and of culture; his whole body and spirit had for the time being committed themselves to that second finger-tip. After having folded the old but well-cared-for pouch, removed the last speck of tobacco from his hands, and restored the pipe to his teeth, he lit a wooden match slowly and unerringly, and sucked with decreasing force until the weed was deeply, evenly afire. The hand holding the match, the muscles of the face working, the eyes blinking slightly, the neck bending – all seemed made by divine providence for the pipe.

When the match was thrown out of the window, and the first perfect smoke-cloud floated about the compartment, only the eye that sees not and the nose that smells not could deny that it was worth while. The dry, bittersweet aroma – the perfumed

soul of brindled tawniness – was entirely worthy
of the pipe. No wonder that the man had con-
secrated himself to this service. To preserve and
advance that gleam on the briar, to keep burning
that Arabian sweetness, was hardly less than a
vestal ministry.

There was not a sound in the carriage except
the colonel's husky, mellow breathing. His grey
face wrinkled by its office, his stiff white moustache of hairs like quills, his quiet eyes, his black
billycock hat, his unoccupied recumbent hands,
the white waterproof on which they lay, his spot-
less brown shoes matching the pipe, were parts of
the delicate engine fashioning this aroma. Certainly they performed no other labour. His limbs
moved not; his eyes did not see the men and
women or the child, or the basketful of wild roses
in her lap, which she looked at when she was not
staring out at the long, straight-backed green hill
in full sunlight, the junipers dappling the steep
slope, and whatever was visible to her amongst
them. His brain subdued itself lest by its working
it should modify the joys of palate and nostrils.

At the next station a pink youth in a white
waterproof, brown shoes, and hollycock hat, carrying golf-clubs and a suit-case, entered the carriage.
The colonel noted the fact, and continued smok-

48

ing. Not long afterwards the train stopped at the edge of a wood where a thrush was singing, calling out very loud, clear things in his language over and over again. In this pause the other passengers were temporarily not content to look at the colonel and speculate on the cost of his tobacco, his white waterproof, and his teeth and gold plate, on how his wife was dressed, whether any of his daughters had run away from him, why he travelled third-class; they looked out of the window and even spoke shyly about the thrush, the reason of the stop, their destination. Suddenly, when all was silent, the little girl held up her roses towards the colonel saying:

'Smell.'

The colonel, who was beginning to realize that he was more than half-way through his pipe, made an indescribable joyless gesture designed to persuade the child that he was really delighted with the suggestion, although he said nothing, and did nothing else to prove it. No relative or friend was with her, so again she said:

'Smell. I mean it, really.'

Fortunately, at this moment the colonel's eyes fell on the pink youth, and he said:

'Is Borely much of a place, sir?'

Every one was listening.

'No, sir; I don't think so. The railway works are there, but nothing else, I believe.'

'I thought so,' said the colonel, replacing his pipe in his mouth and his mind in its repose. Every one was satisfied. The train whistled, frightening the thrush, and moved on again. Until it came to the end of the journey the only sound in the carriage was the Colonel knocking out the ashes of his pipe with a sigh.

THE PILGRIM

THE 'Dark Lane' is the final half-mile of a Pilgrim's Way to St. David's. It may be seen turning out of the Cardiganshire coast road a little north of the city. Presently it crosses the 'Roman road' to Whitesand Bay, and then goes down into the little quiet valley that holds the cathedral and a farm and a mill or two. Travel has hollowed out this descent; bramble and furze bushes on the banks help to darken it. Yet the name of 'Dark Lane' is due rather to the sense of its ancientness than to an extremity of shade. Perhaps on account of the shadow it may cast on the spirits of men it is now little used, unless by the winter rains; and some days of storm had made it more a river than a road when I walked up it, away from St. David's. I looked back once or twice at the valley, its brook – the Alan – its cathedral, and the geese on its rushy and stony pasture. I had no conscious thought of antiquity, or of anything older than the wet green money-wort leaves on the stone of the banks beside me, or the points of gorse blossom, or a jackdaw's laughter in the keen air. If the pilgrims never entered my mind, neither did living people. The lane itself, just for what it was, absorbed and quieted me.

I was therefore disturbed when suddenly,

among the gorse bushes, I saw a young man kneeling on the ground, his back turned towards me. If he had not heard me approaching he knew, as soon as I stopped, that some one was there. He was more surprised and far more disturbed than I. For in a flash I had seen what he was kneeling for; and he knew it. He was cutting a cross on a piece of rock which had been left uncovered by moneywort. Obviously he felt that I must think it odd employment for him on that December day.

He was not a workman carving a sign or a boundary stone, or anything of that sort. He was nothing like a workman, but was clearly a young man on a walk. A knapsack and a thick stick lay at his side. He was dressed in clothes of a rough homespun, dark sandy in colour, good, and the better for wear, and with nothing remarkable about them except that the coat was not divided and buttoned down the front, but made to put on over his head. As he wore breeches he showed a sufficient pair of rather long legs. His head was bare, and his brown hair was untidy, and longer than is considered necessary for whatever purposes hair may be supposed to serve. He might have been twenty-five, and I put him down as perhaps a poet of a kind, who made a living out of prose.

He looked at me with his proud, helpless, blue eyes; his lips moving with unspoken words. He shut the knife he had been using as a chisel, and opened it again. I knew that he would have given anything for me to go on after saying 'Good morning,' but I did not go. I asked him how far it was to Llanrhian, and if the main road beyond here was the original continuation of the 'Dark Lane,' or if part of it was missing, and so on. He answered, probably, by no means as best he could, for he was thinking hard about himself. In a few minutes he could no longer keep himself to himself, but began to talk.

'I suppose you wonder what I was doing, cutting that cross?' he said in a defensive tone.

'Was there an old pilgrim's cross there?' I asked innocently. 'I have heard they carved crosses on some of the stones along the road.'

'I have heard so too,' said he; 'but I have been looking out for them all the way from Cardigan and have not found any.'

'Then you have carved this yourself?'

'Yes; and I suppose you wonder why. Well, I don't know; I can't tell you; I don't suppose you would understand; I am not sure if I do myself; and at any rate it is no good now.'

53

'I hope my interrupting you . . .'

'Oh, no, I don't think so. But when I began I thought it would be a good thing. I got as far as this at daybreak, and I was feeling . . . what is it to you? Seeing this old stone, which is perhaps the last before I reach the cathedral, and no cross on it any more than on the others, an idea came to me. I had been thinking about those pilgrims, some of them with torn feet, some hungry, or old, or friendless, or with an incurable disease. And yet they came here to St. David's shrine. They must have thought there was some good in doing so; they would be better, even though their feet might still be torn, or they might still be old, or hungry, or friendless, or have their incurable disease. But the shrine is now empty. I did think that perhaps the place where the relics used to be, when they were not carried out to battle, would have some power. All that faith would have given it some quality above common stone. But I doubted. Then I thought. "But faith is the thing. If those pilgrims had faith there was no special good in St. David's bones, except, again, that they believed there was." I tried to think in what spirit one of them would have carved a cross. Perhaps just as a boy cuts his name or whatever it may be on a bridge, thinking about anything or nothing all

54

the time, or sucking at a pebble to quench his thirst. At the sight of this stone – I may have been a fool – I thought – I had a feeling that while I was doing as the pilgrims did I might become like one of them. So I threw off my knapsack and chiselled away. . . . Please don't apologize. In any case it would have been no good. The knife was already too blunt, and I was cold and aching and also thinking of a wretched poem. Do you think a pilgrim ever had such thoughts? If there was such a one he would never have got far on his road.'

I tried hard to lure him into a Socratic dialogue to disclose what had brought him so far. He went on:

'The quickest city in the world is St. Pierre, which was overwhelmed by the volcano on Mont Pelée. But one cannot easily become a citizen of St. Pierre. Well, well, what is it to you that I want in some way to be better than I am? I must be born again: that is certain. So far as it is in my power, I have tried hard. For example, there is no ordinary food or drink or article of clothing I have not given up at some time, and no extraordinary one that I have not adopted. There remains only to wear a silk hat and to drink beer for breakfast.

'I have been to physicians, surgeons, and enchanters, but they all want to know what is the matter with me. I answer that I came to them to find out. Then they listen gravely while I tell them about a hundredth part of the outline of my life. They write out prescriptions; they order me to eat more or eat less, or to be very careful in every way, or not to worry about anything. They shake hands, saying: "I was just like you when I was your age. You will be all right before long. Good-bye."

'My family paid a specialist to come to see me at the house once. He and I had the usual conversation. Then he was given lunch, which he ate in complete silence, except for a complaint about the steak. After receiving his cheque my mother asked him rather tragically what to do. "Don't hurry him on, Mrs. Jones," he said, "and don't keep him back, Mrs. Jones."

'For forty days I visited an enchanter continually. He did not promise to cure me, though he also said that at my age he was just like me – which was untrue, for he had a Yorkshire accent. Day after day in his room I sat with closed eyes, repeating "Lycidas," silently with the object of not thinking about anything, especially the incantation. This consisted of a whispered, slightly hesitating assertion that I should get well, that I should be happy, that I should have faith, that I should have no more doubt, but confidence, concentration, self-control, and good sleep. After several minutes I always heard the enchanter take out his watch to see if he had given me enough. From that time until the end I was doing little but listening to the crackle of his shirt-front and cuffs. It was so funny that I was even more serious about it than he; but after forty days I had had enough. My rebirth did not take place in the house of the enchanter.'

'When I was your age . . .' I began; but luckily I was inaudible.

'I have tried many medicines,' he continued. 'I have been to a physician who offers to cure men who are suffering from many medicines. All in vain. I tried a medicine which all great writers take, and which presumably makes them greater or keeps them great; but it had no effect on me – my literary ambition died.'

Here he took out his watch.

'Zeus!' he said. 'I have been two hours at this thing,' and he rose up. 'I must photograph that cross and put it in my book. That will pay for the wasted time.'

He photographed the stone and cross, and

departed with long strides down the 'Dark Lane' before I could ask about his book, but I see no reason to doubt that he was writing a book.

THE FIRST CUCKOO

In each spring, as in each man's youth, all things are new, and the finer our feelings the more numerous and powerful the impressions made on them. As life or the year advances new things appear continually, the old are repeated or varied, both by chance and design; multitudinousness, coupled often with decrease of sensibility, reduces the impressions, in number, in power, or in both. Countless are the things which may impress us for ever. It may be the sound of bells pealing, it may be the smell of glue on a toy dissolving in a hot bath. But the majority fade away or can be revived only by poetry. or strange chance. Very few endure. Those that do, most men are pleased and even proud to recall over and over again.

Usually it is supposed that the first experience makes the lasting impression, and by a kind of natural superstition a special importance is attached to 'first' experiences, even when of a kind that can be repeated. Instinctively, but not unconsciously, we prepare ourselves in a reverent or enthusiastic manner for the first sight of a house or tree or hill which has a meaning for ourselves only. And so with unexpected recurring things of universal significance, like the appearance of the new moon, or of the faint Pleiades in early autumn. Almost every one is pleased to report the crescent moon low in the west on a fine evening: many probably have an exaltation, however faint or indeterminate, at the sight, which they have no idea what to do with. Thus many times a year we enjoy in a milder, more Epicurean way, something like an imitation of a real first experience. I am not forgetting how much of the thrill may be due to the feeling of a fresh start, combined with that of being an old inhabitant of the earth.

But the first cry of the cuckoo in spring is more to us than the new moon. The first flicker and twitter of the swallow is its only possible rival. The first snowdrop, the first blackbird's song or peewit's love cry, the first hawthorn leaves, are as nothing even to those who regard them, compared with the cuckoo's note, while there are many for whom it is the one powerfully significant natural thing throughout the year, apart from broad gradual changes, such as the greening or the baring of the woods. The old become fearful lest they should not hear it: having heard it, they fear lest it should be for the last time. It has been accepted as the object upon which we concentrate whatever feeling we have towards the beginning of spring. It constitutes a natural, unmistakable festival. We wish to hear it, we are eager and anxious about it, we pause when it reaches us, as if perhaps it might be bringing more than it ever brought yet. Vaguely enough, as a rule, we set much store by this first hearing, and the expectancy does not fail to bring its reward of at least a full and intense impression. And for this purpose the cuckoo's note is perfectly suited. It is loud, clear, brief, and distinct, never in danger of being lost in a chorus of its own or another kind: it has a human and also a ghostly quality which earns it the reputation of sadness or joyousness at different times.

When we hear a bird's note for the first time in spring, it usually happens that conditions are favourable. If rain is falling or wind roaring in tossing branches, any noise but a loud or near one may be drowned; also mere cold and cloudiness, if they do not keep us indoors, suffice to put us out of the humour for expecting. Thus only naturalists are likely, as a rule, to hear the 'first' note in conditions which are unfavourable, that is to say, which will not further its effect. Again, if we have minds bent on other things or altogether troubled and self-centred, the chances are against hearing it. Company and conversation, the sounds

61

of men or horses or wheels, have the same effect
as rain or wind. Thus we often first hear the
cuckoo in the first mild, quiet weather of spring,
with minds more or less tranquil. If I hear it so,
though I cannot imagine anyone less superstitious,
I have a feeling of luck. Nine or ten years ago, I
remember hearing the cuckoo sing for the first
time when I had started out for the day. The bird
was slanting down towards our plum-trees and
cuckooing there, so that I could not help running
home in the hope that I should be first to tell the
news.

When I heard it this April, I could not be
wholly absorbed in it, yet something of me was
carried away, floating in a kind of bliss over the
river between the hills. I had been walking all day
in Carmarthenshire in hot, bright weather. But
no mossy lane overhung by ash trees, no little
valley of ivy-mantled oaks or gorse blossoming, no
crooked orchard above the roadside, no bushy,
dripping precipices that echoed to the gulls' cry
on pale sand and white serpentine water, possessed
a cuckoo. One bird I heard for the first time that
morning – a corncrake in a thicket of thorn and
sallow by Goose's Bridge. But at the moment I
had no wish to hear that wooden comb scraped.
It is a sound for the mowing grass, for the height

and heat of midsummer. I was, in fact, irritated by hearing this undesired, unseasonable call already, before the cuckoo's note which I had been listening for during a whole, fine week. Then some hours later I was returning by that same road between Laugharne and St. Clear's. I did not pass one man, woman, or child, for each of the four practically houseless miles. It is a road that rises and falls in following the direction of the Taf, and keeps usually in sight below it the loops of the river, the rushy levels and the low hills opposite, divided by dark hedges with a few red ploughlands and many green pastures, with a scattering of gorse. The corresponding hills crossed or skirted by my road on this side, were similar. The mile between the hills was silent. It being then after seven and the sun having just fallen crimson upon my right, the air was still and cool, the sky cloudless as it had been all day.

The road was deep in dust, but the marigolds in the ditch preserved their brightness and their coolness. Coming over the shoulder of the hill called Pwll y Pridd, by the farm Morfa Bach, where the primroses were so thick under the young emerald larches, I began to have a strong desire — almost amounting to a conviction — that I should hear the cuckoo. When I was down again at

Goose's Bridge, by the brook that descends out of a furzy valley towards the Taf, I heard it, or thought I did. I stopped. Not a sound. I went on stealthily that I might stop as soon as I heard anything. Again I seemed to hear it; again it had gone by the time I was still. The third time I had no doubt. The cuckoo was singing over on the far side of the valley, perhaps three-quarters of a mile away, probably in a gorse bank just above the marsh. For half a minute he sang, changed his perch unseen and sang again, his notes as free from the dust and heat as the cups of the marigolds, and as soft as the pale white-blue sky, and as dim as the valley into whose twilight he was gathered, calling fainter and fainter, as I drew towards home.

THE brothers of great poets are seldom poets: if they are, I believe they are minor poets. But Christina Rossetti, the younger sister of a great poet, became a poet, and not a minor one, and that in spite of the fact that this brother was a very dominating character. It was not that she escaped from the influences surrounding her. She was influenced by the same forces as Swinburne and her brother Dante Gabriel, by Tennyson, by Browning, by the English Bible. Mr. W. M. Rossetti has even said that if 'all those passages which were directly or indirectly dependent upon what can be found in the Bible' had been cut out of Christina's books, they 'would have been reduced to something approaching a vacuum.' And a number of her short narratives are little more than duplications of poems by Tennyson, notably 'The Sisters.' Yet she avoided, on the whole, being derivative and second-rate. She did so, apparently, by reason of her very weakness; if you like, by her femininity. She was content only to do what she alone could do. While Swinburne and her brother forsook the Biblical style, she retained it and made it her own. The poetess who is sometimes regarded as her peer or rival, Mrs. Browning, was more ambitious and energetic; she wrote poems which demand comparison with those of men; and she failed. Christina Rossetti competed with no man. She is, I think, the greatest of the women among our poets.

Her religious, or rather her purely devotional, poetry has to be considered by those whom it practically concerns. The outsider can see only that it appears to excel in emotion and simplicity the work of other poets, such as Quarles, within that field. But in the selection just published,[1] and in Mr. Rossetti's larger one, a good proportion of poems ask no exceptional effort from the outsider of ordinary experience and ordinary acquaintance with literature. He finds himself at once in a region which he may not wish to inhabit, but for which he will find no substitute or equivalent elsewhere, though he will recognize that from it have come colonies not insignificant in later poetry. Had Christina Rossetti never written

> Long ago and long ago
> And long ago still,
> There dwelt three merry maidens
> Upon a distant hill.

> One was tall Meggan,
> And one was dainty May,

[1] In the *World's Classics* series.

But one was fair Margaret,
More fair than I can say,
Long ago and long ago . . .

it would have been a double loss, since it would
have been a loss to the poetry of Mr. Walter de la
Mare.

Christina Rossetti lived a superficially tranquil
and uneventful life, a delicate spinster holding a
Christian faith 'of the most absolute and also of
the most literal kind.' Her work does not bring
us in contact with tremendous or conspicuous
things outside that life, either in Nature or Art or
History. No single poems stand out in exciting
contrast of light or gloom. The gradations up
from her least to her best are so numerous and
slight, her range is so small or her method so subdued, that the effect can be called monotonous, like
that of all religious poetry. To get her full value
the mind must be dissevered both from the motionless opulence of Keats and the light soaring swift-
ness of Shelley. Yet she is both light like Shelley
and still like Keats, without being vapid or slug-
gish. And to say that her range is small is not
quite fair. The fact is that her scale is reduced.
She looks, as it were, already from another world,
and sees children of about the same size as goblins

and somewhat faintly represented, as on tombstones, by their names, Lettice, Rachel, May,
Marian, and so on. By a simple vocabulary, re-
markably frugal of adjectives, and by lucid
rhythms, she produces many different effects,
always of equal firmness and fragility. She refines
things into their essences. Her poems are the unearthly essences, echoes, or reflections, of earthly
tragedy. It is not short lines and little words only
that make 'The Wind' seem a translation out of
one of our poets by an elf:

> The wind has such a rainy sound,
>   Moaning through the town,
> The sea has such a windy sound, –
>   Will the ships go down?
>
> The apples in the orchard
>   Tumble from their tree, –
> Oh, will the ships go down, go down,
>   In the windy sea?

So her repeated sadness is a pretty thing, a sort
of shadowed enjoyment even for the poetess herself, who imagines in death a stillness 'that is almost Paradise,' and is half in love with the sound
of 'vanity of vanities.' She complains, without
bitterness or discontent, of irremediable things,

68

turning them to music. Shadow, instead of light, is her nourishment. Her weariness knows no struggle, hardly even impatience. She speaks, and it is music. As for the reader, he may be as much amused by the Victorianisms in 'Her heart was breaking for a little love' and elsewhere, and in the poem beginning

Sleep, let me sleep, for I am sick of care,

he can enjoy without a pang the roses and myrtles which the sad speaker rejects as well as the poppies and ivy and 'primroses that open to the moon,' which she desires, while he at best receives nothing but delight from

When I am dead, my dearest,
    Sing no sad songs for me . . .
Plant thou no roses at my head,
    Nor shady cypress tree;
Be the green grass above me
    With showers and dewdrops wet:
And if thou wilt, remember,
    And if thou wilt, forget.

I shall not see the shadows,
    I shall not feel the rain;
I shall not hear the nightingale
    Sing on as if in pain;

And dreaming through the twilight
That doth not rise nor set,
Haply I may remember,
And haply may forget.

For hers was an instrument having the power to
make out of little words and common things, including a discontent with this earth and life which
is not too deep for tears or words and 'goes not to
Lethe,' a music more enduring, perhaps not less
monotonous or more really sorrowful, than that of
a larch tree sighing in the wind.

IT is rumoured that Mr. Charles Dalmon is still alive. For the sake of those who do not know that such a man was born, I must premise that he was, some time last century, at Old Shoreham, in Sussex. On his mother's side, he said he was descended from the Vinings of Somersetshire, a family that had manorial rights before Parliament wars against King Charles. He claims descent also from William Damon, the favourite lute player of Queen Elizabeth. He asserted that he had Romany blood in his veins.

But I believe that his life and writings are more remarkable. He worshipped Tennyson, he admired Mr. Norman Gale, and he discovered himself. He was the author of 'Minutiæ,' 'Song Favours,' 'Flower and Leaf,' and several gypsy poems that used to be recited and applauded ten years ago.

Before Mr. Belloc and Mr. Kipling, he was a Sussex poet, and his poem on the old woman who let the cuckoo out of the bag every year at Heathfield Fair is quoted in Mr. Lucas's *Highways and Byways in Sussex*. He saw strange visions. For example, he saw Cupid and two or three other gods down in Sussex, and even in Chiswick he knew a Dryad. She haunted a mulberry tree in an old garden. I do not know whether the Psychical Research Society confirmed this but the poet went so far as to promise her

> An altar made of wood or stone,
> And carven with these words by me:
> The Dryad of the mulberry,
> A goddess very dear to those
> Who worship in this garden close.

Not a poet in England now, though there are several in Sussex and some in Chiswick, says a word about these distinguished foreigners, for I do not count Mr. de la Mare. His 'little old Cupid' with the small broken bow was a mere statue, and so, I expect, was his 'Tired Cupid.' Fourteen years have passed since Mr. Dalmon's last book was published.[1] That short period, then, whatever else has been done in it, is memorable for the second fall of the gods.

If Mr. Dalmon were alive and still writing poetry, and if he were to come to us now saying:

> Between the sunset and the dusk
> Dan Cupid came to me
> Out of a border full of musk,
> Crying most bitterly. . . .

[1] This was written in 1914. Mr. Dalmon has since published two volumes of verse.

we should hardly have a laugh to spare for his presumption of our credulity. Nor would it do for him to urge that the Sussex Muse is a real person, who still

Against the sundial leans and plays
The very tunes she played in bygone days
To Fletcher, Otway, Collins, Shelley, Realf.

But in 1900 it was different. I can believe anything of 1900, and yet more easily of 1895, which was the year of 'Song Favours.' In those days Mr. Watts-Dunton was Theodore Watts, and his poems were still in preparation. Beardsley, Benson, Beeching, Bridges, Buchanan were all in one publisher's list. It was a sort of golden age. Poets had ivory towers full of malt liquors, the blood of the grape, and the works of Tennyson, whom Mr. Dalmon had met. England was still held by some geographers to be Arcady, and Mr. Dalmon addressed himself to –

All those to whom the fields in spring
Are still the fields of Arcady.

Perhaps the fact was already in dispute, for by 1900 Mr. Dalmon employed a tone of pleading, if not of doubt:

O, never say that Pan is dead
And every nymph and satyr fled.

73

But essentially he was a poet neither of doubt nor pleading, but happy and clear, and his peculiar happiness and charm of utterance sprang from a reunion of the pastoral and the rustic, of Flora and Hodge. His poems were 'bits of ribbon and bits of flower.' Not content to give England some of the attributes of Arcady, he enriched Arcady with the birds and flowers, and some of the sweetest place-names, of England, particularly of the Weald and the Downs. While Cupid walked between his lovers 'the goldfinches sang in the sloe trees.' This combination was his chief characteristic. In one of his drinking songs he bids the host to put rose leaves in the beer. He delights to picture Pan at the Epiphany. Christ, the gods, and the fairies keep company in his books.

In his day there were milkmaids in England, and one named Phyllis. His poem called 'Milking Time,' where she is mentioned, is one of the most perfect examples of Mr. Dalmon's mingling of what is rustic with what is pastoral and literary. The feeling is Arcadian, the detail English:

Come, pretty Phyllis, you are late.
The cows are crowding round the gate.
An hour, or more, the sun has set.
The stars are out; the grass is wet;

74

The glow-worms shine: the beetles hum;
The moon is near – come, Phyllis, come.

The black cow thrusts her brass-tipped horns
Among the quick and bramble-thorns;
The red cow jerks the padlock-chain;
The dun cow shakes her bell again,
And round and round the chestnut tree
The white cow bellows lustily.

The last verse really seems to prove that Mr.
Dalmon knew what he was talking about when
he used the word 'faery':

Now faeries, fays, elves, goblins, go
And find out where she lingers so,
And pinch her nose and chin and ears,
Nor heed her cries, nor heed her tears;
At any farm 'twould be a crime
To be so late at milking time.

In his day men used to drink beer for pleasure,
not to spite the teetotallers. Mr. Dalmon drank,
and when he was not thirsty wrote poems about
it, which are the best possible of their kind. There
is 'Cider Apples,' which opens:

Some choose to worship in the church;
   Some choose to worship in the chapels;
But we will worship by ourselves
   In orchards full of cider apples.

75

ought CR

One of his last hymns for that sect is –

All earthenware is dust and clay,
　And dust and clay is ev'ry man;
And if you can't be easy, well,
　Just be as easy as you can.
O, some have thin Venetian glass
　From which to drink their foreign beer,
But give us cups of Barum ware
　And cider made in Devonshire.

And among statelier pieces there is 'The Song of Favonius':

The flagon topped with foaming ale
Invokes the song and faery tale,
And he who sings the sweetest song
To him the flagon shall belong
The silver flagon richly chased
With hops and barley interlaced;
But he who tells the fairest tale
More than the singer shall prevail,
For he shall win the prize divine,
The fragrant kiss of Proserpine.

Mr. Dalmon could be stately and he could be roguish. But he did not mix the two kinds. They seldom did in those days. Only he puts his 'Joyous Gard' between his merry 'Sloes' and his genial 'Autumn Allegory':

76

'The hazel nuts are slipping in the lane' . . .

In his day Camelot and Joyous Gard were mighty names. In his day, too, it was possible to flatter a lady by saying that when she came out on a dull day, the sunflowers turned towards her, etc., and although I don't believe they did, I would rather Mr. Dalmon told the lie than anyone else born since Waterloo.

HAMPSTEAD HEATH IN AUGUST

HAMPSTEAD HEATH is too good in itself to be made or obliterated by associations. When you have gone up nearly to the top of Heath Street – put in a certain humour by oldish, quiet shops, and flagged pavement in place of asphalte – you forget Keats and Leigh Hunt, 'Arry and 'Arriet and Mr. Kipling. The street goes steep and straight up to perhaps the highest point of the heath, and when you are almost there the walls of the last pair of houses frame the milky blue of the high harvest sky. Then, suddenly, they seem the last houses in the world; for only a hundred yards of ground lies visible between you and the sky.

This patch, containing a pond, is of hard, dry, bare, undulating gravel like a sea beach, and because nothing is to be seen beyond it save the unclouded blue, it creates instantly and powerfully the belief that beyond the edge of this beach the sea is hidden, whether at the foot of a cliff or of a gradual slope is uncertain. The belief lasts a quarter of a minute, and once at the top of the street and on this bare patch, the horizon is seen to be not a curve of sea, but serrated woods upon a long line of hills, all swiftly revealed as if by a

79

miraculous command at blast of trumpet. Almost
in the same moment, over the edge, the hollow
land of the heath appears below you. Houses un-
mistakably bound it. Sometimes they look over it
as if they regarded it as a possession. Sometimes
as if they felt some dull astonishment at being
separated only by the road from these billowy trees
and wild hollows.

Were the heath level, this sense of possession
would be lasting and complete. But the uneven
wildness due to nature and excavation makes up
for its small extent and saves the heath from the
humiliation. Thus the houses are nothing but a
frame: they do not combine the heath; they neither
influence it nor receive any influence from it. They
stand bald and impotent at the edge of this fragment of the wild. They are indifferent to the dry
air, spiced with harvest, which divides all the little
leaves of the trees and carries the bright notes of
swallows and scattering linnets.

The last sheet but one of August Bank Holiday
paper has been picked up. The dust, though harsh
to feet and eyes and nostrils and fingers, is sweet
to the mind because it is the dust of summer, and
the linnets sweeten it like a fount breaking out of
dry sand. This wind, though soft as sleep, is one
of the great winds of the world: it touches the

cheek with the tip of a light wing dipped in coolness, though the air is as fiery as it should be at St.
Bartholomew-tide. It is no mere afterthought
from the first illusion of distant sea : this August air
extends from sea to sea over the world, linking the
streets and these suburb glades to the upland corn,
league beyond league, and to the waves shimmer-
ing around the coast.

ICKENHAM IN SEPTEMBER

IT was a low grass country, resembling in character
one of those round ponds, quiet and shady, where
eels and tench are to be caught and on Sundays
the farm-boys go bathing. At seven o'clock the
new-risen sun, bursting through the oak leaves,
made a perfect spider's web of silver rays. Sky
and earth were misty. The grass-blades and
bramble leaves were dewy grey, the dandelion
clocks were all over diamonds, at the edge of the
dusty road: the elderberry bunches hung heavy
and drenched above them. The woods, one field
distant, were vast homes of darkness and silence
and what else I knew not, but certainly something
more, roofed with innumerable yellowing leaves.

In the gardens the populations of great and
lesser sun-flowers, dark crimson dahlias, red roses,
pale hollyhocks and Shirley poppies yet paler, all

looked as if they had somehow just streamed out of the gloomy cottages whose doors stood wide open – so happy were they in the first sunlight; while the purple crocuses of Autumn seemed but then to have broken out of the underworld, a little band of fugitives, and trembled affrighted in their pallor amid all the gorgeousness of the flowers of red and gold.

Over all was a sky, milky blue at darkest, but mostly a soft, dusky white, and without a cloud. The early smoke towered up straight above the chimneys, as blue as the sky. The robin sang alone now in the old crooked orchard, now in the green lane where nettle and dock had multiplied under the hedgerow trees, elm, ash and maple. There was not a soul in sight except the robin, and the mist and the quietness made his tender song seem a requiem, not merely of leaves falling and summer fading, but of all life that had been upon the earth. If all else were peacefully dead, never to rise again, thus would the bird sing.

The robin had the churchyard all to himself – except of course that I was with him. The yew and the elms and limes were motionless down to their lightest leaves while he sang, and I walked round the little ivy-covered church with short wooden spire, and looked at the tombstones of people named Hollywood and Treadaway, very old-sounding and very rustic names, that looked more at home in Ickenham churchyard than over a shop or in most other places nowadays.

Then some one began to work the pump by the little pond of the village, three workmen went by towards Ruislip, and the robin flew down like a leaf into the ivy which enveloped one railed-in tomb. Nothing of this tomb was visible. I suppose it was a tomb: but on that morning if it had not been for prejudice, I should have guessed it rather to hide the entrance to a subterranean world, the world out of which had risen those pale Autumn crocuses, and into which the multitudes of the earth, until a moment ago, seemed to have gone down to tranquillity. I did not investigate. Lying so near the Metropolitan Railway and the Ruislip road, it is safe from anyone's curiosity except the robin's. That bird disappeared there, and after I went out and followed the road winding like a river between its ash trees and elms and oaks, anything might have happened in Ickenham churchyard.

RICHMOND PARK IN NOVEMBER

THE turf in Richmond Park atones for the walls and fences, the gates, the keepers, the regulations, the Royal residence. Wimbledon Common, where every one can do practically as he pleases, day and night, and where nearly everybody does, has nothing like this turf. Any son of man, I believe, except a gipsy following his profession, or a naked savage, is admitted into Richmond Park, and yet nowhere has the grass disappeared or become mangy; even well-used paths are still green.

This is due to the fact that there is a Presence always in the park. No doubt this Presence will be explained away by some who believe in the omnipotence of Royalty, deer, and entrance gates; but these things do not wholly explain it, either for Royalist or Republican. The dignity and perfection of these few miles of open country are as repellent to some as they are attractive to others: no one will deny the Presence.

The combination here of the uncultivated and the refined is a beautiful one. Nothing could be purer and freer than the long clear levels, the flowing gradual rises of rushy and ferny turf – the buff oak-woods on the higher places, with clean-curved borderings of bracken – the companies of glowing beeches or elms here and there, and of crimsoned hawthorns, big and old, like those in Savernake Forest, – often to be seen without one human visitor, while the green woodpecker laughs astonishingly, and the stags fence and roar under the trees. Yet nothing, to experienced eyes, could be more plainly due to refinement, depending on generations of forethought and protection, and judicious neglect.

Few can complain of the enclosures which preserve thickets in untouched abundance. They are to the park what the park is to the outer world. They are citadels of quiet. Their palings give opportunities for adventures to the adventurous: for the rest there is the pleasure of looking in on these secret, secluded little provinces, all the sweeter for being out of reach, except of the mind, and of the squirrels and the birds, the pied chaffinches chinking all through the November day as they flit, the single thrush, singing his mild November song in the poplar that has four yellow leaves left at its point, the robin mysteriously warbling, mysteriously silent, mysteriously rustling among the dead leaves.

Richmond Park has all the qualities of other parks, the unploughed undulations, the old trees, irregularly but happily scattered, the winding, well-kept roads, the cloistered wilderness, the deer, the squirrels, the jackdaws, the notice-boards; but they appear to be in greater perfection, because the walls keep in the deer and the peace, but keep out London. Of course, they keep out other things, so that in a sense the park is only half real, as if it were under a glass-case. Without the glass-case, however, it could not exist; it would be destroyed by the life which it now excludes or converts.

HARROW-ON-THE-HILL IN DECEMBER

FAR away and high up the sky of morning is blue, its clouds are white, but under them travels a loose, dirty scud, letting fall momentary showers at intervals. The earth glimmers with myriads of little pools; the trees are very black, and the green and gold of moss is bright among the branches. In the shadowy and nevertheless clear air, under the ghost of a moon, thrushes are singing with sharp voices. They seem to sing away the drift and the showers, and presently all the sky is pure except for a procession of mountainous clouds along the horizon, having grey sides and snowy summits, which are obliterated southwards by the December sun in a blaze of white; and Harrow-on-the-Hill, and St. Mary's hilltop spire among its elms and lime-trees, stand up hard and bold in the midst of a land gleaming with innumerable pastures, interlaced and bounded by dark trees that were many of them not young when Byron

looked out over them from Peachey's grave in the
churchyard. As for London, it is a pale and silent
conjectural city under that misty blaze of the sun.
Looking away from London across the spread of
country which a straight railway instead of a winding river pierces, hardly a house is visible until
after the eye has returned from the distance and
condescended to look just below, beyond the foot
of this green hill. There lie the villas of Harrow –
the dairy-farms among their elms and horse-chest-
nuts – Roxeth village, with its plain old cottages,
a gasometer, and a small inn called 'The Timber
Carriage,' belonging, I suppose, to the period of
the tomb in St. Mary's, where John Henry North,
a judge of the Admiralty in Ireland, 'without a
superior in chaste and classic eloquence in Parliament,' lies buried. That wide country of elm and
oak still needs timber carriages, if not chaste and
classic eloquence in Parliament. For eastwards
rank beyond rank of round-topped trees, on land
gently rising to the horizon, combine into one
wood, streaked by a few strips of meadow. And
there absolutely not one house can be seen. A
solitary crow steers for it: he sinks among the
trees with a croak as if he were the only being
alive in all that woodland. The houses immediately about me and the nearness of London are not

merely powerless for the moment to spoil the
solitude of this crow's landscape at fall of night:
they intensify the unexpected solitude, because
they make it seem improbable, fantastical. But it
does not pass away or change; it becomes part of
the deep night of many stars, while the houses
themselves are the unreal, hollow, transitory
things, and London a foreign city of ghosts.

KEW GARDENS IN JANUARY

ON an ordinary crowded afternoon the gardens
at Kew are like a museum of all the trees and
plants written by the Creator. There is something
incongruous and intrusive in the rustle of leaves
and the song of birds, something awkwardly and
astonishingly unofficial in a shower of real rain.
But in January the trees rebel: they refuse to
admit that they are safe-locked in a museum.
They are no longer self-conscious and peaceful
about their labels. The Scotch fir forgets that the
heather was planted at his feet by order. The
silver lime has lost her shyness of the fact that in
summer she has one low small branch where all
the leaves are three times the normal size – next
year perhaps it will be different. The deciduous
trees seem glad to have cast off their best clothes
that used to make them quite at ease with the

pretty dresses of ladies strolling amongst them. With their naked boughs, dark and hard, they utter wintry noises as if they had formed a conspiracy to act the parts of trees at liberty – as if the beeches were among a thousand companions on the steep slope of a down, the elms out in an undulating meadow in a friendly cluster, and the ash-trees overhanging a mountain roadside. The birds haunting them are also freer to-day, when the west wind is mild and the sun gentle in a bower of grey clouds. The whistle of the nuthatch, solitary in the top branches, makes the elms happy. The ash is flattered by the great tit that hangs so long on its twigs, saying 'Chittabob,' and then over and over again, 'I'll wait a bit . . . I'll wait.' The beech knows well that it is right for a green woodpecker to rush laughing loudly into its arms. When the fir has a band of starlings piping together on its crest it is an exile no longer. The hawthorn has its bullfinch and is comforted. The bold challenging song of a missel-thrush persuades all but the palms that the tropical glass-house is an illusion which must fade when the sunlight ceases to glitter on it. To-day the grassy glades are not mere straight green streets. They have a wildness, completed by a light and already half-melted fall of snow. They would not resent a Gypsy camp and

89

camp fire in place of a nursemaid and silken children. They lead the eye out to a sunset sky as yellow as silk in the cocoon, or down to the Thames where willows are blowing and the water is rippled all over like a file. To-day the river is not, as it sometimes is, a rude contrast to the ordered gardens, but it gives another touch, like the west wind, the clouded sky, and the birds singing, to the liberty of the winter trees. When I have gone out and the gates are closed, the conspirators are silent, dark, and happy in the twilight, as if they were thoroughly assured that with the night all will be well with them, and their dreams are to be confirmed for ever.

IN times of peace and tranquillity the vocabulary of patriotism is not much used. The old songs are sung occasionally without question; in speeches, lectures, and leading articles, where men are licensed, the old forms are repeated. Many a man who is at all particular about meanings of words leaves alone patriotic and religious phrases, with or without a reservation that there are times when they have meant something and will mean something again. Trouble changes this. The most touching phrase of patriotism in *The Anglo-Saxon Chronicle* occurs where the chronicler, writing, I imagine, amid the troubles of the Conquest, records the death of Edward the Confessor. He speaks of Edward dwelling in exile while 'the Danes wielded the dear realm of England.' When Edward the Martyr was murdered at Corfe Castle the chronicler remarked: 'Never was a worse deed done to the English than this was since they first sought Britain.' If England lies like a vast estate calm around you, and you a minor, you may find faults without end. If England seems threatened you feel that in losing her you would lose yourself; she becomes plainly and decidedly 'this dear realm of England'; if you are in exile you may understand how the Roman Emperor in the *Mabinogion*

had Roman earth brought to Britain that he might
sleep, sit, and walk upon it and keep in health.
The old phrases come back alive in war-time. I
have heard a farmer's wife refer to England as
She. At an ordinary time Henley would say:
'Beef, beer, horses, *Moll Flanders*, and the Church
of England, the King, and the *Newgate Calendar*
– what is there, what could there be more typically
English than these?' But writing *Pro Rege Nostro*
the same man saw England 'with glorious eyes
austere, as the Lord were walking near,' and
addressed her as –

> 'You whose mailed hand keeps the keys
> Of such teeming destinies. . . .'

In print men become capable of anything. The
bards and the journalists say extraordinary things.
I suppose they do it to encourage the others.
They feel that they are addressing the world;
they are intoxicated with the social sense. But
it is a curious thing that they do not talk like
this in private, or I am exceptionally unfortunate in meeting the wrong sort of bards and
journalists. In a newspaper a bard, and a
young one, will address 'The "Nut" who did
not go': –

'You're a hero bold,
  My gallant son,
Though you do not hold
  A soldier's gun.
For you wave a little flag
Which is quite a bally fag,
Though, perhaps, it is a "rag"
And rather fun.'

But I never happened to hear bard, journalist, clergyman, or woman using this kind of patriotic phrase in private. I have heard a man say, 'The soldiers are splendid, aren't they? Aren't they all splendid?' I heard a woman say: 'I don't quite know what they mean by England. Sometimes I feel proud, but more often ashamed, though certainly I can't say there is any other country to which I would rather belong.' And I am not sure that love of country can go much farther in words, except under the influence of alcohol or a crowd; that is, among those who only stand and wait. It is, perhaps, curious also that I never was in company where any man or woman said that somebody else ought to enlist. When they have expressed an opinion, soldiers and civilians have said that they cannot understand anyone pointing out his duty to another. I do not conclude that 'my country' and the like are literary phrases, and that men no more use them in real life than they call their mistresses 'Lady' in the style of bards of the 'nineties; but I understand the temptation to this conclusion.

While I was trying to learn from other people what they meant by 'England' and 'my country,' I went to a friend who knows his England and is not ignorant of Europe. I did not say, 'Why do you love your country?' but I must have used words to that effect. I wanted to know what he felt. Instead he told me what he thought, now that I asked him. He said: 'What quaint idea is this? Reasons why I love England? Do I love England? If I *prefer* England I expect it is merely that I am accustomed to it, that my material welfare is bound up more or less with that of the whole country, that the greater number of beautiful sensations I have enjoyed are associated with its scenery and its people. These reasons would hold good for any other country, if I had chanced to be born elsewhere.' (He carelessly forgot that if he had been born somewhere else he would have been a different person, and so on.) 'In any case these reasons are not sufficient to make me conscious of any active love of England, in the sense that it would be impossible for me to be quite as

94

happy in any other country – excepting always the loss of old associations.' (He forgot to consider how much he possessed apart from associations.)

'All my material interests are here, and since the war started I have frequently been in a blue funk that I should be left destitute.' (He forgot to consider how much that would matter, if associations counted for comparatively little; for his country would have provided him with food, drink and shelter.) 'So I am patriotic – in the sense that I want the Germans to be smashed.

'I am conscious most of my love of myself; that is, not self-approval, but a *constant* solicitude as to my getting and doing what I like and what I think good for me. Are not all Western people like this? We love ourselves, not our country. If I owned a bit of land I think it might make a great difference to my feelings.' (Here is a chance for a landowner who wants to manufacture patriots.) 'But I don't own any, and in common with the forty-four millions of the dispossessed, I know that I am never likely to. The dice are cogged against us by the capitalists and other cunning monopolists, who, in their turn, love no country but only what they own in it.

'I listened yesterday to a prosperous middle-aged man bullying a booking-office clerk, because our fast evening train from town is temporarily suspended. He was furious about it, as it would mean the loss of, say, half an hour every evening to him. What did he care that the Government wanted extra railway accommodation for a time, in order to ship troops and ammunition in huge quantities? All he was conscious of was that his habits would be interfered with, his dinner a little late every evening.

'This man is a patriot. He says so himself. He has an immense contempt for any enemies of England, and his ignorant, blatant jingoism is an offence to any decent man who happens to share the same compartment in the train with him.

'Are there other, finer kinds of patriots? I don't know them. If by patriots we mean men who wish good to their own country at the expense of no matter what other country, I hope not. For such patriotism is only a high-sounding name for self-interest, self-preservation.' (He forgot that this was what he himself was chiefly conscious of. He was capable of anything, in this mood for applying superhuman standards to everybody.) '*My* instinct is to apply to the whole world Marcus Aurelius's words: "That which is not for the interest of the whole swarm is not for the interest of a single bee."

'In the present crisis I distinguish. I think the

good German peoples have been mistaught and misled. Their moral standard is lower than that of their enemies; their victory would mean re-action. I want them, for the sake of the whole world, to be beaten.'

I am sure nobody that he or I would bother about can question his patriotism. But he was eager to dissociate himself from sentiment which he thought false. He is a stickler for the meanings of words. 'Love of England' seemed to him to mean so much that he denied it to himself and apparently to most others. Being naturally a just man he tried to be supernaturally just with his head. Fortunately I knew even more of his feelings than can be gathered from his last sentences. For example, when he was abroad, he was frequently shocked by the table manners of foreigners, and although he is not supernaturally squeamish in conversation when it is a question of amusement, I remember him condemning the French severely because they used as a technical term for a certain machine, and in print, too, a word invoking an obvious gross image. An Englishman would laugh at the image. A Frenchman was not ashamed to use it seriously, and was condemned for it by the Englishman. Also, I have heard this same man say that often he can't

help feeling that our men are the best in the field,
though he is anxious not to be deceived by that
sort of talk. That is to say, he prefers England
and English ways when it comes to a comparison.
It would not be rash to class him with the other
man who said that England was a place where 'one
isn't forbidden to do what one wants to do or
forced to do what somebody else wants,' and that
in spite of gamekeepers; for who ever met a
landowner in a wood?

I take this to be the foundation of patriotism. It
begins with security. When a woman with a child
could cross the country safely patriotism began to
be certain. Before that, England was 'the island of
Britain,' 'the land of the English race,' rather than
England, though 'England' was used almost as
early for this island as 'Britain,' and the two terms
are mixed in the early Chronicle as in the
authorized version of the French Yellow Book,
which says: 'The statement regarding the inter-
vention of the English fleet is binding on the
British Government.' The poem on the Battle of
Brunanburh speaks of Edward the Elder's sons
defending 'our land, our treasure, and our homes.'
In the poem on the Battle of Maldon, the earl
facing the Danes with his levy says they will
defend 'this homeland, the country of Ethelred

my prince, the people and their ground.' Here already is what Wordsworth expressed for the Tyrolese: –

'The land we from our fathers had in trust,
And to our children will transmit, or die:
This is our maxim, this our piety;
And God and Nature say that it is just!
That which we *would* perform in arms – we must
We read the dictate in the infant's eye;
In the wife's smile; and in the placid sky;
And, at our feet, amid the silent dust
Of them that were before us. – Sing aloud
Old songs, the precious music of the heart!
Give, herds and flocks, your voices to the wind!
While we go forth, a self-devoted crowd,
With weapons grasped in fearless hands, to assert
Our virtue, and to vindicate mankind.'

By the time of the Battle of Maldon men had long possessed and often defended irreplaceable things in England. Out of England the same men would have had nothing unless they had a sword. They had begun to realize that without England they were little or nothing: that with England they were 'greater than they knew,' since, according to their strength and their affection they were part of what Milton says a commonwealth should

99

be, 'one huge Christian personage, one mighty growth and stature of an honest man, as big and compact in virtue as in body.' Men forgot that the English race came once upon a time to Britain and made it England. They were preparing to think of Britain as rising out of the sea at Heaven's command, with the sovereignty of the sea, as Edward the Third says in Blake's play: –

> 'That Heaven gave
> To England, when at the birth of nature
> She was seated in the deep; the ocean ceased
> His mighty roar, and fawning played around
> Her snowy feet, and owned his awful Queen.'

Two little things in early English history suggest England more vividly to me than bigger things. One is the very stunted hawthorn round which the battle of Ashdown mainly clashed, between the Danes and King Ethelred with his brother Alfred and the Christian host, 'fighting for life, and their loved ones, and their native land.' Two kings and five earls of the 'pagans' fell there, says Asser, who tells the tale; and he had with his own eyes seen the tree. Incidentally I know by this that the Berkshire down-top there by the Ridgeway was no more wooded then than it is now. But above all it tells me of the making of landmarks and the beginning of historic places. Of such things has England gradually been made, not lifted at one stroke by Heaven's command out of the azure main. The other little thing is the hoar apple tree where Harold's host met the Conqueror near Hastings. Here I have a foretaste of the England of Chaucer and of Langland, who, in one book, could speak confidently of such widely separated parts of England as London, Walsingham, Banbury, and the Malvern Hills, and of so many parts of London as Cornhill, East Cheap, Shoreditch, Stratford, Tyburn, and Southwark. There was a man, half-Londoner, half-Worcestershireman, and all Englishman. Even so was Walton, three centuries later, half-Londoner, half-countryman, as he shows in many a passage like this: – 'When I go to dress an Eel thus, I wish he were as long and as big as that which was caught in Peterborough river in the year 1667; which was a yard and three-quarters long. If you will not believe me, then go and see at one of the coffeehouses in King Street in Westminster.'

Many of the early kings and earls, in the same way, were partly Kentish or Hampshire men, partly, on great occasions, Englishmen. Already, before Langland, a Gloucester man, Robert of

Gloucester, had called England 'merry' in his chronicle: —

'England is a right merry land, of all on earth it
    is best,
Set in the end of the world, as here, all in the west.'

It was the Merry England of the English people, 'full of mirth and of game, and men oft-times able to mirth and game, free men of heart and with tongue.' Whether it would have seemed Merry England if Robert had been writing in Sussex or Northumberland is not certain. For I take it that England then as now was a place of innumerable holes and corners, and most men loved — or, at any rate, could not do without — some one or two of these, and loved all England, but probably seldom said so, because without it the part could not exist. The common man was like a maggot snug in the core of an apple: without apples there are no cores he knew well, nor apples without cores. Giraldus Cambrensis put this beautifully in speaking of his birthplace, Manorbier in Pembroke. Demetia, he said, was the most beautiful as well as the most powerful part of Wales, Pembroke the finest part of Demetia, Manorbier the most delightful part of Pembroke: 'it is evident, therefore, that Manorbier is the pleasantest spot in Wales.'

Throughout English history you have the two
elements combined inseparably, love of the place
where you 'have your happiness or not at all,' and
a more fitfully conscious love of the island, and
glory in its glories. On the one hand Edward
Leigh, who lived a hundred years in the sixteenth
and seventeenth centuries, quotes at the end
of his advice to travellers these words of Sir
Benjamin Rudyard: 'France is a good country
to ride through, Italy a good country to look
upon, Spain a good country to understand, but
England a good country to live in.' For an Englishman England was the snuggest place under
the sun, and he imagined it made for him like
a house. Cowper called it the Heaven-protected
isle –

'Where Peace and Equity and Freedom smile,
 Where no volcano pours his fiery flood,
 No crested warrior dips his plume in blood. . . .'

Everything centres round such an isle. Wordsworth calls the evening star, seeing it from Calais
as it sets over England, 'star of my country.' To
Hazlitt England was the place for bells and non-
sense. 'Bells,' he says, 'are peculiar to England';
and 'I flatter myself that we are almost the only
people who understand and relish *non*sense.' Eng-

land was, for Blake, 'the primitive seat of the Patriarchal Religion': for (or therefore) –

'All things begin and end in Albion's ancient Druid rocky shore.'

On the other hand, there is a more active patriotism of comparison and aggression. The patriot scorns other lands which he does not know and could not live in: he delights to discover and assert that foreigners living in different houses on different food are inferior to his countrymen. Raleigh answers the question whether the Roman or the Macedonian were the better warrior by saying: 'The Englishman.' But stay-at-home Englishmen treat their neighbours across the bridge or the hill not much better. The Wiltshireman says that Hampshire is where they held the pig up to see the band go by; and the Hampshireman says that Wiltshire is where they buried the donkey on his back with his feet out of the ground so that they could polish his shoes. The very villages have been honoured thus by satirical neighbours: Aldbourne in Wiltshire is where they tried to drown the moorhen, and Wroughton (I think) is where they gave the pig a watch to see when it was time to eat.

A happy nation luxuriates in its differences and

distinctions, as a county does in its Selsey cockle, Chichester lobster, Arundel mullet, and Amberley trout. The people of such a nation can taste and enjoy the patriotism of another people, like the Tyrolese, or a bygone patriotism defeated in its own land, as Wordsworth did the patriotism of the Ancient Britons: —

'Mark, how all things swerve
From their known course, or vanish like a dream;
Another language spreads from coast to coast;
Only perchance some melancholy Stream
And some indignant Hills old names preserve,
When laws, and creeds, and people all are lost.'

The more differences a nation has had freedom to preserve or to develop, I should say, the greater the variety of affections it will concentrate from time to time, and as civilization advances the more complicated will be the affections felt towards it by those who know more than one or two holes and corners, by those with the purest culture. There comes a thrill, to-day at least, on hearing so complete an Englishman as Walton say out of the fullness of his knowledge that 'certain fields near Leominster, a town in Herefordshire, are observed to make the sheep that graze upon them more fat than the next and also to bear finer wool; . . .

which I tell you, that you may the better believe
that I am certain, if I catch a trout in one meadow
he shall be white and faint, and very like to be
lousy; and, as certainly, if I catch a trout in the
next meadow, he shall be strong, and red, and
lusty, and much better meat.'

Englishmen are more different from one another than from foreigners who all seem alike: they
will quarrel together like husband and wife who
know one another's weaknesses yet will turn as
one upon the outsider who interferes. For we have
gone so far in security, and the idiosyncrasy and
pride born of it, that we can criticize and attack
not only one another but even the whole, which is
at one time a jealous God and at another a kindly
nurse; there is no need to be always blindly shouting like schoolboys at a football match.

I suppose a time comes when shouting and
waving a flag is the best or only thing worth doing
if you are not being shouted or waved for, when
one of our national growths, men or ideas, has
triumphed. For if there is a patriotism that does
not lose its savour by being carried too far over
the sea it is one like Milton's where he first praises
'the stout and manly prowess of the German dis-
daining servitude; the generous and lively im-
petuosity of the French; the calm and stately

valour of the Spaniard; the composed and wary
magnanimity of the Italian,' and then beholds 'the
nations of the earth recovering that liberty which
they so long had lost; and the people of this island
transporting to other countries a plant of more
beneficial qualities, a more noble growth, than
that which Triptolemus is reported to have carried
from region to region, disseminating the blessings
of freedom and civilization among citizens, king-
doms, and nations.' In time of war the differences
get sunk, though still one regimental band plays
'The Lincolnshire Poacher' and another 'Ap Shen-
kin'; and either we see or fancy some one of our
virtues, our beefsteak or our liberty or our regard
for small nationalities, being acknowledged in a
practical manner by the enemy; or we become
excessively conscious of our weaknesses, misdeeds,
shortcomings, as Coleridge did when he was in
fear of an invasion in 1798, or as Mr. Horatio
Bottomley does in the lines: –

'Come, comrade, we must answer – and let our
answer be –
Why is the red blood flowing? – *To chasten you
and me.*'

But right or wrong, if it is a question of existence,
it is hardly easier for a man to imagine his country

beaten down than to imagine himself dead, and I have heard reasonable, anxious, and careful men say they never have any doubt that we shall win.

A writer in *The Times* on patriotic poetry said a good thing lately: 'There may be pleasanter places; there is no *word* like home.' A man may have this feeling even in a far quarter of England. One man said to me that he felt it, that he felt England very strongly, one evening at Stogumber under the Quantocks. His train stopped at the station which was quite silent, and only an old old man got in, bent, gnarled, and gross, a Caliban; 'but somehow he fitted in with the darkness and the quietness and the smell of burning wood, and it was all something I loved being part of.' We feel it in war-time or coming from abroad, though we may be far from home: the whole land is suddenly home. Wordsworth felt it in the valley near Dover immediately after landing in August, 1802, when he wrote the sonnet beginning: –

'Here on our native soil we breathe once more.
 The cock that crows, the smoke that curls, that sound
 Of bells; – those boys who in yon meadow-
     ground

In white-sleeved shirts are playing; and the roar
Of the waves breaking on the chalky shore; –
All, all are English. . . .'

Some books can give the same feeling. I took up
the *Compleat Angler* the other day, and felt it there.
Since the war began I have not met so English a
book, a book that filled me so with a sense of
England, as this, though I have handled scores of
deliberately patriotic works. There, in that sort
of work, you get, as it were, the shouting without
the crowd, which is ghastly. In Walton's book I
touched the antiquity and sweetness of England –
English fields, English people, English poetry, all
together. You have them all in one sentence,
where the Milkwoman, mother of Maudlin the
milkmaid, is speaking to Piscator and Venator:
'If you will but speak the word, I will make you a
good syllabub of new verjuice: and then you may
sit down in a haycock, and eat it; and Maudlin
shall sit by and sing you the good old song of the
"Hunting in Chevy Chase," or some other good
ballad, for she hath store of them: Maudlin, my
honest Maudlin, hath a notable memory, and she
thinks nothing too good for you, because you be
such honest men.' They are all in two sentences of
Piscator's: 'And now look about you and see how

pleasantly that meadow looks; nay, and the earth smells so sweetly, too. Come, let me tell you what holy Mr. Herbert says of such days and flowers as these, and then we will thank God that we enjoy them, and walk to the river and sit down quietly, and try to catch the other brace of trout': then he quotes Herbert's —

'Sweet day, so cool, so calm, so bright. . . .'

This man knew England and the men who knew England best — Camden and Michael Drayton. Drayton, the author of *Polyolbion* and the ballad of Agincourt, was Walton's 'honest old friend.' There is one other passage which I shall quote, though my subject is not the *Compleat Angler*, because it reminds us how much a man may be lord of that he does not possess. He is speaking of some fields which belonged to a rich man with many lawsuits pending, yet he who 'pretended no title' to them could take a sweet content in them: 'For I could sit there quietly, and looking on the water see some fishes sport themselves in the silver streams, others leaping at flies of various shapes and colours; looking on the hills, I could behold them spotted with woods and groves; looking down the meadows could see, here a boy gathering lilies and ladysmocks, and

there a girl cropping culverkeys and cowslips, all
to make garlands suitable to this present month
of May: these and many other field-flowers so
perfumed the air that I thought that very meadow
like that field in Sicily of which Diodorus speaks,
where the perfumes arising from the place make
all dogs that hunt in it to fall off, and to lose their
hottest scent. I say, as I thus sat, joying in my own
happy condition, and pitying this poor rich man
that owned this and many other pleasant groves
and meadows about me, I did thankfully remember what my Saviour said, that the meek possess
the earth. . . .' I believe the man who thought it a
'quaint' idea to love England would feel very much
as I do about these passages and about Walton
altogether. I believe that England means something like this to most of us; that all ideas of
England are developed, spun out, from such a
centre into something large or infinite, solid or
aëry, according to each man's nature and capacity;
that England is a system of vast circumferences
circling round the minute neighbouring points of
home.

TIPPERARY

To the tune of 'It's a long, long way to Tipperary' I have just travelled through England, from Swindon to Newcastle-on-Tyne, listening to people, in railway carriages, trams, taverns,
and public places, talking about the war and the
effects of it. They were people, for the most part,
who worked with their hands, and had as little to
do with the pen as with the sword. The period
was from August 29th to September 10th,[1] when
everybody in town and village, excepting as a rule,
the station-master, was discussing the transport
of Russian troops down the country – 'if they were
not Russians, then they were Canadians or else
Indians,' as a man said in Birmingham. I shall
write down, as nearly as possible, what I saw and
heard, hoping not to offend too much those who
had ready-made notions as to how an Imperial
people should or would behave in time of war, of
such a war, and while the uncertainty was very
dark. For their sakes I regret that men should
everywhere be joking when our soldiers were
fighting and our poets writing hard. Though not
magnificent, it is war. At Coventry a fat man
stepped stately off a weighing machine. Seventeen
stone, accumulated in peace. A lean man with a

[1] 1914.

113   H

duck's-bill nose at once attacked him. 'You're the sort of man that stays behind, while a lot of fine young fellows go to fight for their country. I suppose you stay to take care of the ladies. When the Kaiser reaches Coventry he'll see a lot like you. You ought to be ashamed of yourself. You will be.'

Every one had his joke. The porter who dropped something and caused another to jump, covered up his fault by exclaiming, 'Here come the Germans.' Precisely the same remark was made when small boys let off crackers after dark. The hostess with the false hair, being asked if her husband had gone to the war, and how she liked the idea of his being in Paris, replied with a titter that she did not fear – 'the gay girls have all left Paris.' More serious, but not more satisfactory, were the thousands of young men streaming away from the football ground at Sheffield on a Saturday afternoon. Yet even at a football match recruiting can be done and the hat sent round. Some professionals were paying five per cent. of their wages to the Relief Fund, as men in a number of factories were contributing 2*d*. or 3*d*. a week. And a man in blue overalls said to me in Birmingham, 'If a man doesn't fight, he will do better to go to a football match than to drink in a pub or stay indoors moping.' On the other hand, everyone seemed to acknowledge that the war was the great thing; at the free library a hundred shuffling coughers were studying war to one that concentrated on Aston Villa.

The most cheerful man I met was reading *The British Weekly*, and continually saying rotund and benignant things. 'The Irish,' he would pronounce, 'have responded manfully. In fact, this unfortunate business has bound people together more than anything else could have done.' A young Northumbrian recruit was the most wretched. He had walked twenty-six miles to enlist. 'I wish to God I was back again in the village,' he said, 'though it is a cock-eyed little place. Since I came here I haven't had a wash or a brush or changed my clothes. If I were you I would sit farther off. I have had a cement floor for a bed, and some of them singing till three in the morning. We have to be out at six. The food's all right, but it's worse than a dog's life. I wish I could get back, and I will too.' Here a recruit of slightly longer standing, and already wearing a uniform, cut in with, 'I wish I had your chance, I'd be off. We have been moved fifteen times since July.' 'You'll be all right in a day or two,' said a decent, wooden-legged man, flicking away this fly from the jam of patriotism.

Most men fell short of the recruit in wretched-
ness and the reader of *The British Weekly* in
benignity. Unless the Kaiser was mentioned they
used, as a rule, the moderate language of sober
hope or philosophic doubt. The one act of
violence I witnessed was an oldish man, with a
head like a German Christ, knocking down a sot
who persisted in saying, 'You look like a –
German.' More typical was the man I overheard
at Ardwick, talking of the black and white pig he
was fattening for Christmas, regardless of the fact
that the Kaiser had God 'magnificently supporting
him.'

Wherever I went I was told that employers –
'the best firms' – were dismissing men, the
younger unmarried men, in order to drive them to
enlist. 'Not exactly to drive them,' said one, 'but to
encourage.' Nobody complained. They suggested
that the 'Government' had put the employers up
to it, or that 'It don't seem hardly fair,' or 'It
comes near conscription, and only those that
don't care will give up good wages and leave their
wives to charity.' One old man at Sheffield remarked that it used to be, 'Oh, you're too old' for a
job; now it's 'You're too young.' It was added
that the men's places were to be kept open for
them; they were to receive part of their wages;

if rejected by the doctor, they would be taken back. 'They *have* to like it,' said one man. These were not the only men who had lost their work. The jewellery-makers of Birmingham, for example, young or old, could not expect to be employed in war-time. Collieries near Newcastle that used to supply Germany were naturally idle, and many of the lads from these pits enlisted. Factories that supplied Russia were not busy either, and Russian debts looked like bad debts. Some trades were profiting by the war. Leicester was so busy making boots for the English and French armies that it had to refuse an order from the Greek army. Harness-makers had as much work as they could do at Walsall. The factories for explosives at Elswick the same. Publicans were flourishing though still ambitious; one public-house at Manchester had these 'Imperial Ballads' printed on a placard: —

'What plucks your courage up each day;
What washes all your cares away?
What word do you most often say?
Why, Imperial!'

the reference being to a drink of that name. But these successes were extraordinary. Already it was said at Newcastle that shop-assistants were serving for longer hours at reduced pay. Men in motor-car works were on short time. A photographer at Manchester had to resort to this advertisement: –

'Gone to the front!
A beautiful enlargement of any photo of our
brave comrades may be had at a discount of
25 per cent.'

Where relief was being given, a queue of women stood along a wall in the sun.

For the women the sun was too hot, but not for the corn, the clover-hay, the apples, of this great summer, nor for the recruits sleeping out. The sun gilded and regilded the gingerbread. Everybody that could, made an effort to rise to the occasion of the weather. The parks and the public gardens were thronged. The public-houses overflowed, often with but a single soldier as an excuse. Bands played in the streets – at Newcastle bagpipes – to quicken recruiting. A crowd listened to a band at Birmingham outside the theatre before going in to hear Mr. Lewis Waller recite 'Kipling and Shakespeare,' and the first remark to break the ensuing silence was, 'It's by far the best band in Birmingham, by far.' Street meetings having no connection with the war were held. Men in the Bull Ring at Birmingham one afternoon argued furiously on faith and works, quoting Scripture amid eager onlookers. At the top of Oldham Street, Manchester, two knots of men on a Sunday evening debated what would or would not happen under Socialism, while one in the centre of a looser knot shouted, 'Oh, my friends, God wants all of you.' The war, in fact, was the one subject that was not debated in public. A man breaking this rule was branded a Socialist. For instance, near the statue of James Watt at Birmingham a man had got into an argument about the provision for soldiers' wives. Moistening dry lips with dry tongue, he declared that the working class made fifty times the sacrifice of the upper class. He met nothing but opposition, and perhaps only persevered because he was wedged tight among his enemies and could not for ever keep his eyes downcast. At length a vigorous elderly man in a grey suit stepped in with fists clenched, said he was a working man himself, and laid it down that every one's business was to fight, to sink class, and to avoid quarrelling. His wife, smiling behind him, told the heretic that he ought to be ashamed. Someone chipped in, saying that as a matter of fact many wives were better off with their one-and-twopence than when the men were working. 'God help them before!' ejaculated the solitary man. Then another said he was going himself, and would go if his wife was penniless. 'Hear, hear!' said several; and others muttered, 'These here Socialists.' Of course, class feeling did exist. A workman in Birmingham hoped that not too many of the well-to-do would go to the front, because they were needed to give employment and to control it. The rich and the working-class, said a Coventry man, were doing their duty, but not the middle class – he called it the 'second class' – 'these young fellows who are neither man nor girl, and think about their socks all day.'

The war was not debated, but every one was bound to turn into it as into a main road of conversation, bound also to turn out of it. It could not be avoided. The newspapers issued edition after edition without reason. Pavement artists were strong on admirals, generals, and ships. Portraits of General French and Admiral Jellicoe adorned the entrances to picture palaces. Some one had chalked on a pavement at Manchester: 'See no sports. Fight the good fight.' Young men going to work by train began talking about the Russians. One interjected that he *was* glad to receive his salary in full at the end of the month. Another looked up from his paper saying, 'Kitchener's getting his second hundred thousand.' A

Socialist was quoted as having said that 'we might as well be exploited by Germans as by British.' Gradually they drifted into stories about public men, into indecent stories about anybody, until running into a fog at Birmingham one exclaimed: 'It's a bombardment. We must be careful what we do and say to-day. It's a warning.' Older men going out to the Peak for Sunday, zigzagged from fishing yarns to 'uncreditable' tales told by a German in the Secret Service, on to the moorland appetite that makes you eat three-quarters of a pound of ham at a meal, and back again to 'I haven't had a day off except Sunday since the war began.' 'You durstn't.' The street roar of Newcastle or Sheffield was compounded of hoofs, boots, wheels, gongs, a thousand voices interwoven and one shouting, 'Fourth edition,' one whispering, 'If Turkey . . .'

Conversations definitely on the subject of the war, fed on the abstract diet which the Press provided, were much of a muchness. A man began reading: 'This bloke says the rapidity of the German advance on Paris fairly stupefied the French,' or he reminded his friend that 'this war has often been predicted in this very place.' A man interrupted his game of dominoes to say: 'I thought before now we were going to cut the

German communications.' A man stands silent for a long time among his mates, and suddenly blurts out: 'What I want to know is, are these bombs' (he means mines) 'made of iron?' A favourite opening was, 'There's some great move coming.' The end of a conversation about the retreat was: 'The English have always been cool, calm, and collected.'

All kinds of abstract legends were current, as that the Germans were cowards, that the Kaiser was mad; but not many concrete ones. There was the Russian legend. Then there was a tale earlier in the war that British wounded were arriving at Grimsby, and the town was like a shambles. One man actually in Grimsby, answering an inquiry on the telephone, said that this was so; but another was able to deny it on good evidence.

One of the legends was that England was careless and slack. In the levelling of this charge I think there was a certain fondness as well as indignation. Men liked to think that we could play bowls and win a battle in the same day. 'England is too good-hearted,' said a man at Swindon. He came into the bar asking for 'Down where the water-lilies grow' on the gramophone, and, being disappointed, he sighed and began to speak of his 'month of misery'; for he had three sons and five nephews, or, as he sometimes put it, five sons and three nephews, at the front. 'The English are too good-hearted. Here, look 'ee. If any damned foreigner comes into this bar we give him a penny as soon as if he was an Englishman. Now I thinks and studies a lot. You recollect the manœuvres at Faringdon? Well, there was all nations there, Germans, Italians, Russians, French, Egyptians, and I don't know what – fifteen nations. Do you think they wasn't taking notes? Of course they were. And the Kaiser – the mad bull – didn't he come over and kiss King Edward, and wouldn't he as soon have knocked him down?' There was a man at Birmingham who began by talking about the Russians and Ostend, two millions of them, he believed. Oh, yes, they had certainly come down through England by night. He thought the Russians would repay the Germans for their atrocities. Nor do I think he minded. Yet he drew satisfaction from the faith that the English themselves would not retaliate. No, he said, the English are 'easy.' A Sheffield man who was advocating the bloodiest treatment for the Kaiser said that, 'If English soldiers fired at the Red Cross, Lord Kitchener would blow their brains out, he would.' Men were bloody-minded, to judge by their talk. They would have

123

had no patience with the gentle person who had his favourite horse shot to save it from the battle-field. More intelligible to them would have been the gentleman of Cromwell's time who sent orders to have the sucking foals slaughtered that the mares might become chargers.

Such men had a strong, simple idea of a per-fidious barbaric Germany. 'They have been pre-paring for this war ever since old Queen Vic died, and before that. I'd turn all the Germans out of England, same as they would turn us out.' 'I wouldn't; I would shoot the lot of them.' 'These nationalized Germans – you don't know what they are up to. Double-faced, they're all double-faced. They're savages, killing children and old men. I'd like to get at the Kaiser. I wouldn't kill him. I'd just turn him loose. . . .' 'I wouldn't. If I could get at him, I'd . . . and choke him with them.' Thus spoke two workmen in Coventry. An old woman at Swindon – one of thousands – wanted to 'get at the Kaiser.' Everywhere men were drinking health – with a wink and 'You know what I mean' – to the Kaiser or the 'King of Proosher.' A very sober workman of fifty in New-castle who was working short time simply did not know what epithets to give the man, and had to relapse on 'that tinker' (with much expression).

Almost the only judicious reference to him that I heard was: 'Either the Kaiser is mad or he has found a new explosive.' People varied a little more in their attitude towards the German nation. 'They have got to be swept out of Europe,' said a man at Sheffield. A gentle old man was going to Harrogate with 'nerves run down' and 'distorted views,' and he had got it into his head that he had eaten a German sausage. The man with *The British Weekly* was consoling him: 'Oh, you may depend upon it, it did not come from Germany. There's nothing coming from there now. They make a great quantity at Leeds. They don't call it German sausage either.' A Tyneside Scot, after pronouncing the Kaiser mad to make war on 'all nations,' said: 'The Germans are a rotten lot. They won't stand and fight like any other nation. They keep moving all the time.' Others regarded the German army as a sort of ridiculous bully and coward, with this one grace, that it would probably shoot the Kaiser. A few praised German strategy and organization. One youth at Manchester even ventured to think 'they must be a fine race of soldiers.' A man at Sheffield held up a pair of German nail-scissors, lamenting that now he could not buy anything so neat at fourpence-halfpenny. A man at Manchester was asking: 'Where shall we get our gas mantles?' It was a Coventry man who went so far as to say that the German people were as good as ourselves and not so very different. 'They don't want war. It's not the Kaiser either. It's the aristocracy. Still, the Kaiser must not come here, like other deposed monarchs.'

This man, like every one else, was sure of victory. Some expected Paris to fall, but . . . They only laughed at any doubter. Most held the opinion that in retiring on Paris the Allies were leading the enemy into a trap. They did not stomach the idea of English soldiers retiring and retiring, and they imagined it must be deliberate. Open boasting had gone out of fashion, unless the man is a boaster who says on a black day that an Englishman is equal to five Germans. Patriotism took subtler forms. It was reported that one of the new Territorials weighed nineteen stone. 'Oh, but he will soon lose four or five stone, don't you fear. It's a healthy life, a grand life.' 'What I most rejoice at,' said a man at Swindon, 'is that we did not want the war.' Scores said something like it. It was 'the greatest war of all time,' said all sorts of people. In Sheffield a solitary pessimist was content to think it the ruin of Europe, a great sudden movement in 'evolution.' The dirtiest man in Sheffield, with the most rasping voice, talk-

ing among his mates on a Saturday afternoon
about rights of way, dukes, corporations, trespass-
ing, and poaching, jerked out the remark: 'The
capitalist is forking out now to save his own
property.' A printer in the same town said: 'We
are not soldiers or politicians; we are workmen.
We have our trades, it is not for us to fight. That
is another trade: let the soldiers fight. That is
what I used to say; but it won't do now. All I can
say is that I don't feel like fighting, myself. There
is a great deal of loyalty everywhere, and I hope
we shall win.'

Peace was not much talked about. A man at
Swindon was figuring a reconstruction of Europe
after the war. 'Why,' he asked, 'why shouldn't all
the countries be bound together like the United
States? There are a lot of nationalities over there,
and they agree very well, I fancy.' Probably many
were using the same phrases as the Birmingham
chess-player: 'The pity of it, when you think of
all the education in England and Germany. *We*
don't go out into the street and fight if we have
a difference. It sets a bad example to the nation.'
'It's man's nature to fight.' 'It isn't mine.' 'Your
move.'

Only one eloquent militarist did I hear, a Manchester Irishman. He, too, declared it man's

nature to fight. From Cain and Abel, having demolished and labelled as un-Christian the suggestion that we were descended from monkeys, he branched out to the animals. 'It's the same everywhere,' he said. 'They must hit out. Until they have hit out, they don't know themselves. To hit out is a man's very life and nature, the best he can do, his greatest pleasure, what he was made for. Most of us have to obey the law, if we can. But the soldier is a hired law-breaker and murderer, and we must let him enjoy himself sometimes. Don't you go pitying the poor soldier. Poor soldier! This is the time he has been waiting for. He is in a passion, and nothing hurts him. Sudden death is a glorious thing.'

This was not a soldier. He was a workman, a looker-on, one of the thousand loitering workers and unemployed who stare at the hundred recruits between the statues of Watt and Edward the Seventh at Birmingham, and in squares or by-streets all over the country. The soldier has another style. A crippled pensioner at Birmingham said simply that if he was fit they would not have to call him twice; then he gossiped of the Burmah war, of catching and killing your own mutton before eating it, of an immortally tough bullock, of having a foot cut off by a Dacoit, of how far better off to-day's soldier is with his bacon and jam and tea for breakfast. A soldier's father at Swindon just said his son was glad to go, but wished it had been with Buller. These were men who would not be hurt till they were struck, and I do not know how much then. The Irishman was not one to squander himself on a battlefield; his duty to his country was to preserve his tongue without having to hold it. But he was a patriot.

Probably there are two kinds of patriot; one that can talk or write, and one that cannot; though I suspect that even the talkers and writers often come down in the end to 'I do not understand. I love.' It must happen more than once or twice that a man who can say why he ought to fight for his country fails to enlist. The very phrase, 'to fight for one's country,' is a shade too poetical and conscious for any but non-combatants. A man enlists for some inexplicable reason which he may translate into simple, conventional terms. If he has thought a good deal about it, he has made a jump at some point, beyond the reach of his thought. The articulate and the inarticulate are united in the ranks at this moment by the power to make that jump and come to the extreme decision. I heard a mother trying to persuade – pretending she was trying to persuade – a young

man against enlisting. She said: 'I would not risk
my life for anybody. It isn't yours, for one
thing. Think of Mary. I would sooner go to
America. . . .' She found a hundred things to say,
few of them quite genuine, since it was her desire
to overpower him, not to express herself. In
argument he was overpowered. His reasons he
could not give. Nevertheless, if he passed the
doctor he was going; if the doctor rejected him,
he rather hoped some girl would taunt him – she
would have to produce a champion to justify her.
Had the eleven or twelve thousand recruits from
Birmingham written down their reasons, I dare say
they would not have been worth much more than
the pen, ink, and paper. That is, assuming they
included no poets, and I do not see that they were
more likely to prove poets than the men, women,
and children who made haste to send in their
verses to the papers. Out of the crowd at Newcastle the dissatisfied one spoke best. If any at
Coventry or elsewhere were kept waiting so long
outside the recruiting office that they changed
their minds and went away, they might speak
better still. Some men of spirit may have kept
back to spite their interfering persuaders. Why,
the lowest slut in the town, fetching her beer at
eleven-thirty, would look after a procession of

recruits and say: 'So they ought to. Lord! look
what a lot of fellows hang about the corners. They
ought to fight for their country.'

There was really no monotony of type among
these recruits, though the great majority wore dark
clothes and caps, had pale faces tending to lean-
ness, and stood somewhere about five foot seven.
It was only the beginning, some thought, of a wide
awakening to a sense of the danger and the re-
sponsibility. Clean and dirty – some of them, that
is, straight from the factory – of all ages and
features, they were pouring in. Some might be
loafers, far more were workers. I heard that of one
batch of two hundred and fifty at Newcastle, not
one was leaving less than two pounds a week.
Here and there a tanned farm labourer with lighter-
coloured, often brownish, clothes, chequered
the pale-faced dark company. The streets never
lacked a body of them or a tail disappearing.
Their tents, their squads drilling this way and
that, occupied the great bare Town Moor above
Newcastle. The town was like a vast fair where
men were changing hands instead of cattle. The
ordinary racket of tramcar and crowd was
drowned by brass instruments, bagpipes, drums
and tin boxes beaten by small boys, men in fifties
and in hundreds rounding a corner to the tune of

'It's a long, long way to Tipperary.' Thousands stood to watch them. With crowds on the kerb-stones, with other crowds going up and down and across, with men squatting forward on the pavement, it was best to have no object but to go in and out. The recruits were the constant, not the only attraction. The newest ones marching assumed as military a stiff uprightness as possible. The older ones in uniform were slacker. Some stood at corners talking to girls; others went in and out of 'pubs' attended by civilians; more and more slouched, or staggered, or were heavy-eyed with alcohol. Everyone was talking, but the only words intelligible were 'Four o'clock winner' and 'It's a long, long way to Tipperary.' At nightfall the boys who beat the drums and tins began to carry around an effigy and to sing 'The Kaiser, the Kaiser,' or

> And when we go to war
> We'll put him in a jar,
> And he'll never see his daddy any more.

Companies of recruits were still appearing. Perhaps their faces were drawn and shining with drink, fatigue, and excitement, but they remained cheerful even when a young officer with a dry, lean face and no expression said 'Good night' without expression and rode off. His was the one expressionless, dead calm face in the city, the one that seemed to have business of its own, until I crossed the river and saw the women on the doorsteps of the steep slum, the children on pavement and in gutter. They were not excited by the fever in Clayton Street and Market Street, any more than by St. Mary's bells banging away high above slum and river, or by the preacher at the top of Church Street bellowing about 'the blessed blood of Jesus Christ.' In an almost empty tavern a quiet old man was treating a lad in a new uniform, and giving him advice: 'Eat as much as you can, and have a contented mind.' It was a fine warm evening. But what could the great crowd do to spend its excitement? As a crowd, nothing. In a short time it was doubled. For at nine o'clock the public-houses had to be emptied and shut. The burly bell of St. Nicholas tolled nine over thousands with nothing to do. Those who had not taken time by the forelock and drunk as much as they would normally have done by eleven, stood about aimlessly. A man took his stand in Bigg Market and sang for money. It was not what people wanted. Several youths got together at a short distance and tried to bawl down the singer. Even that was not what people wanted. Even the temperance man was only half pleased when he reflected that what he had long agitated for in vain had been done by one stroke of the military pen. There was nothing to be done but to go to bed and wait for the morning papers.

IT'S A LONG, LONG WAY

'ALL the other nations are coming in, Canada, India, and . . . They wouldn't let England be beat. Oh, no, sir. England will win, right enough, you'll see. Oh, yes, sir.' An old Gloucestershire labourer was speaking, who had fought under Roberts. He had been at Kandahar, over his boots in blood. East and West, he had had glimpses of many nations; his geography was but the battered remnant of a few infant lessons in Crimean days. When he tried to enumerate 'all the other nations' he had to stop at 'Canada, India.' Russia was in his mind, but as an enemy: he spoke of the Russians when he meant the Germans.

I should like to be able to draw a map of the world as it appears to him. It would be easy enough to make one very picturesque, more than mediæval, with strange gaps, and removals and bringings near; but it would be all wrong, because he does not see the world as reduced to a flat, coloured surface; all he knows is earth, sea, burning sun, India, China, Gloucester, the Malvern Hills, the Severn. Those who can do something with maps go as far astray. One woman who had been expecting friends from Canada was inclined to think they could not reach England, because the North Sea was closed by mines.

135

I should like to know what the old soldier meant by 'England,' if it was anything more than some sort of a giant with Gloucestershire for its eyes, its beating heart, for everything that raised it above a personification. His was a very little England. The core and vital principle was less still, a few thousand acres of corn, meadow, orchard, and copse, a few farms and cottages; and he laughed heartily over a farmer's artfulness who had hid away some horses wanted by the War Office. If England was against Germany, the parish was against Germany, England, and all the world. Some of his neighbours, not so fearless, went even greater lengths in their parochialism. They had made up their minds about invasion. They not only imagined themselves suffering like Belgian peasants, but being specially attacked in the Forest of Dean by German aeroplanes. Napoleon, a hundred years ago, was expected to sail up the Severn and destroy the Forest: now it was feared that the Germans were coming.

The scale of the war baffles country people as it does war correspondents. They take hold of some simple fact and make what they can of it. A woman coming from the town stops you to tell the news – she adds that it is official – that twenty thousand Germans have been killed and another cruiser sunk. The two things have already combined; she does not know whether those twenty thousand were killed on land or sea. Then the arrangement of 'all the other nations' took them aback at the start, and probably still does. It seems a new-fangled notion to have our troops in France fighting for, not against, the French. Perhaps this is considered an heretical innovation by a Liberal Government. The farmer's wife says 'France' with a haughty coolness towards the lady of that name: she had not anticipated such a travelling companion. So when she is really disturbed and is entertaining the idea that it is the Kaiser's 'hambition to eat his Christmas dinner in London,' she says: 'If the Germans try to beat us, the United States will join us.' Very slowly they are readjusting the old multiplication table, which said:

One Englishman = three Frenchmen.

Before the war the word 'Frenchman' had stood for something as distinct and venerable as the Bank of England or the Derby. The word 'German,' in spite of 'The King of Prussia' and 'General Blucher' here and there on a signboard, meant little or nothing. It was almost in vain that the newspapers had been erecting a German Colossus to terrify us. Neither the country people nor their newspapers had read Mr. Charles M. Doughty's 'Cliffs.' They had not listened to the spying Prussian aeroplanists on the East Coast saying of Turkey: –

'We've barely gotten her goodwill, till now.
Yet having that, it is a Key of State.
Be as be may, it costs no more to us
Than promises; and that's only paper-breath.
To us all's one, Muslem or Galilean;
So there's but profit or *Welt-politik* in it . . . ;'

or, worse still, attacking our national songs: –

'Ignoble taunting songs, which they call *komisch*;
Jigging malicious street banality;
Wherat all fleer like hounds and show their teeth;
But hounds should howl to hear them in our parts.'

Nobody knew how old shepherd Hobbe, Crimean veteran, had set upon the spies with his crook, crying: –

'Knives and mailed-fist been cowards' terms with
    us,
For murder-tools of them low foreign seafolk,
On England's quays. Belike ye're some of them,
Would kick an honest man below the belt:
That   bayonet   wounded   soldiers   on   the
    ground. . . .'

On the East Coast, of course, by this time they know what a German is. They have begun to scent a new reality in the old proverbial prophecy: –

> 'When England's took,
> 'Twill be at Weybourne Nook.'

One fisherman who quoted it was being advised, if the Germans landed, to leave fighting to the soldiers, and not endanger the women and children by private efforts.

'Ef I see a Jarman coming up that gangway,' said he, pointing to the cliff, 'do ee know what I'd do? I'd shoot 'm.'

'But –'

'I'd *shoot* 'm.'

Away from the coast the German is not of necessity a devil and a bogy pure and simple. One morning, as I was leaving a lodging at Brecon, and had my hand on the latch, the woman of the house drew me back to know what my opinion of the war was, what was really happening in France, with all these men going out. She also feared invasion. 'I am an active woman,' said she, 'busy all day with my head and hands. What should I do if they cut off my hands?' I told her I did not believe it was part of the German plan to cut off the hands of women, that it was all exaggerated to blacken the enemy. 'That's what I tell my husband,' she said; 'if it was true it would be such a stupid thing to do, to cut off working people's hands. Now, last summer, I had some Germans in this house, and they were nice, polite people, you couldn't wish for better. And look what our own people will do, in times of peace, too.' She was trying hard to retain the idea that there were Germans and Germans.

This woman would not have taken kindly to spying on possible spies. Nor, I think, would many other country people. But once it got about, in a certain part of Gloucestershire, that a Dutchman had been staying in one house, that an American family lived in another, that a party (including a Russian boy) had arrived by motor-car at a third in the middle of the night, all sorts of people joined in the hunt – the policeman, the retired clergyman, acting on the principle that 'you never know what these naturalized Americans are,' and the illiterate anonymous senders of reports that we sat up late at night. People in a country road, nowadays, look hard and sometimes wisely at the stranger passing them. The cottager, however, does not easily regard himself as the policeman's assistant. It is the villa resident that tracks out your alien schoolmaster like a sleuth-hound, and bestirs himself with the police long before the law does. The cottage woman in the Hampshire hop-garden was far less savage than the townswoman. She never saw a newspaper. News came along somehow like fine days, and she knew that far-off battles were being fought, and men dying night and day, in foreign places. When she was told precisely that the Germans had lost several thousands the day before, she said: 'Well, what I say is, God bless every mother's son of them.' Another, more sophisticated, hearing of Germans slaughtered by the bayonet, went so far as to suppose that they also have 'human feelings as we have.'

It may be my misfortune, but I have not heard any abuse of the Kaiser or the Germans, worth mentioning, from country people. Stories of mutilations have reached them. They have met somebody in Petersfield market who saw a soldier in hospital at Guildford, mutilated in the style of William Rufus. Only, they make a short story of it. I was travelling with a drunken hussar to Woking. He had fought at Omdurman, but was in a condition to forget the date. Lying back in a corner seat, he talked to nobody in particular, with a grin for everybody, that is to say, for those sitting in the other three corners. Most of the time he had it his own way, complaining of slow trains, arguing against compulsory abstinence, threatening Lloyd George, trying to figure out the date of Omdurman. Later on, two women entered, and sat facing one another in the two middle seats, one a small, middle-aged woman, bright and demure, with a kind of pretty plainness, the other a buxom wife of thirty. The soldier grinned at them with the sarcasm: 'Don't you sit near me.'

'Oh, I'm not afraid of you,' said the young one, smiling.

'I'm not afraid of you, either,' said the middle-aged one, who was on his side of the carriage. She looked at her knees with a twinkle, but as demure as ever, while she added: 'But I know some one who is.'

'Who's that?' the soldier asked, almost eagerly.

'The Kayser,' she said, still looking at her knees, but as bright as she was demure.

'Ah,' he said, 'the Kayser won't let me get near him.'

'I wish he would,' she concluded.

Outside the towns they see little of the papers; they are not quick at using insubstantial words; they catch few newspaper phrases of the grand style to stand between them and facts. More

natural to them, if anything, would be words like
Mr. Doughty's, in 'The Clouds': –

'That Love of Country, which constraineth us,
Doth every virtue comprehend. Teach us
The very fowls, which under heaven flit,
And field and forest beasts, after their kinds.
Those tender each, that little round of Earth,
Where they were fostered. And should English-
    men not
Their island Britain love, above the World?'

Mr. Hardy makes the soldiers sing: 'We see
well what we are doing.' But those who are left
behind in the hamlets do not know what to make
of big things, or to put them into words. One boy
I talked with, whose brother had joined the Royal
Horse Artillery the day after war broke out, said
chiefly that his brother was now quite fond of a
wild horse, and that he looked much better in uniform than in civilian clothes. He added that they
had paid four pounds a sack, all but three shillings,
for wheat to sow, which was a great price. If they
can make anything of the sinking of an English
ship, at least their conversation profits little by it.
On the Sunday morning when the loss of the
Hermes was published, I was at an inn where I
had formerly met sailors. Opposite Colonel –'s

house, down the street, hung a list of sailors and soldiers from the village, and a frame on which the Colonel posted up telegrams. But the landlord laid down the paper on the counter, saying: 'A cruiser sunk in the Straits of Dover,' and not a man commented. After a pause, the conversation turned to a job that an old man present had just got, of driving a milk-cart at fifteen shillings a week. Not that the war was wholly neglected. One of them mentioned a certain recruit. 'He looks a regular Tom Thumb,' said the spokesman; 'you'd think he'd seen ten years' service. But it's all uniform. It will give the Germans encouragement to see him coming along. Now, at Longmoor Camp, some of the German prisoners are fine-set-up chaps, with something in front and behind, not like this little Tommy Thumb.' After this they wandered, as they often do, to speaking of old days, when they were working on the church out at – , when old – kept the 'New Inn,' and there was a baker's shop where the smithy is now, and – , who is superintendent of police down at the opposite corner of the county, was policeman – he was one for a bit of fun; he would do *anything* that was right.

If the soldiers see, they do not say, what they are doing, One day I had two lads for travelling companions, one a bright, pale, thin boy, with round shoulders, whom I should never have taken for a soldier. But as the train ran between some oak woodland, he waved towards a copse, and said to the other lad: 'That's where I was keeper before I enlisted.' No more; and the other said nothing. Only an old soldier in the carriage asked: 'Terriers?' 'No,' he answered, 'Regular Army. Twelve years. Seven with the colours. Go to Reading on Thursday.' Their farewells are brief. On the night when the hooter at Swindon announced the war at a quarter to eight by hooting ten times, I heard a soldier struggling through his farewells. They were continually being renewed for the sake of a young sister who would burst out crying at the last moment. Just as he said: 'Well, good-bye, Aunt. Good-bye, all,' she screamed, and he had to say: 'I'm not going away for ever, don't you fret. Now, don't carry on like that. I shall come back again.'

In two hours spent at an inn one Sunday with a company of labourers and a young fellow from the village, now a 'Flying Corpse' man, I heard only one reference to the war. 'Regular Winchester Fair weather,' said one, coming in out of the rain, and soon they were guessing the weight and price of some steers across the road, and the one who

was glibbest recalled his master being offered
thirty-two p'n ten for a beast and refusing it, and
then getting twenty-nine and a crown at Winchester market. Most of the time they were re-
calling old days; how they did a job at –, and
slept at the 'Rack and Manger,' taking up a gallon
of beer to the bedroom, and the landlord's wife
kept them company, and in the morning the landlord drove to a farm for eggs, and they had eggs
and bacon. They talked of bacon lofts, open fire-
places, fire-dogs, logs that burned for two days
after Christmas, mushrooms that grow with the
moon – always at night, as you can see by noting
one at nightfall like a button that will be as big
round as a tumbler in the morning – and 'waste
as the moon wast-es,' and mead – 'I'll get you a
bottle. I know where there is some, and I think
it's three year old.' One man mentioned Sparsholt. 'Which Sparsholt?' asked a stranger, who
knew the neighbourhood as well as any. ''Tother
side of Winchester.' 'I know. That's the place to
hide from Germans.' They laughed. It was the
one reference. Yet the paper was lying on the
table. Later on, a youth entered, and bent over
the song printed on the outer page, but said not a
word. The 'Flying Corpse' man was content to
treat his old friends. At half-past two, the one

nearest him said: 'Let's come and see about that pig.' 'Are you going to kill a pig?" asked the youth. 'Going to eat a bit of one.' The 'Flying Corpse' man put a bottle of stout in each pocket, and all left. The afternoon turned fine, and as I approached the town, the girls, in their best dresses, were walking among the dead leaves, but not a young man with them.

This lack of eloquence does not mean a stupid waiting for a drop in the price of bacon. One day I fell into a company talking very radically, and chiefly because they had some thousands of recruits encamping near them and did not like their ways. Some of these recruits had enlisted for 'hunger,' some for fun, not all to serve their country. So said the landlord, an old soldier. 'I wouldn't enlist for anything,' said a man with his cheese waiting on his knife-tip, 'not unless I was made. I would if it was a fair war. But it's not, it's murder. Waterloo was a fair war, but this isn't.' 'That's right,' said the postman; 'a man's only got seventy years to live, and ninety per cent. don't get beyond fifty. I reckon we want a little peace. Twentieth century, too.' It was not the postman, but another, that was complaining how a number of postmen had gone out, and their places had been taken by a few boys in civilian dress who did twice as much work for half the pay, and on their own cycles: 'It's the same everywhere. The man who does most work gets least pay. Nobody's worse paid than the men doing all the work out in France now.' This man, unlike the landlord, was down on the gentry, did not think they were doing their share. He told a story of a lady stopping a youth in a cart to ask him why he was not fighting. Why, he asked, hadn't she sent out her two sons from college? She couldn't spare them, she answered. At his conclusion, 'My mother can't spare me,' the company laughed violently.

In one place I thought I had stumbled on treason. A truculent recruit in the private bar and a drunken old artilleryman were arguing over a dozen heads and tankards.

'We're not fighting for Lord Kitchener,' the artilleryman said slowly. 'We're not fighting for King George. We're fighting for our country.'

'Quite right,' said somebody.

'Who is Lord Kitchener?' asked the artilleryman, swelling.

'He's a good man,' retorted the recruit.

'So he is,' the other had to say, 'but why does he stop a man from having a pint of beer?'

'It's the twenty-fifth pint he's against.'

This was a purely intellectual duel, a very uncommon one. The countryman fights with no such grand motive on his tongue as a journalist could write down. Even the little boys know that, and are not so mighty serious as to be ashamed of laughing when the gawky Territorial shambles down the street in his scarlet tunic for the first time. But the trumpet, a little later, stings them to another mood. The recruits are drilling on the shore in mist, opening and closing, in ghostly silence. For their feet make no sound on the sand, and the calm sea, sucking at the rocks, drowns the shout of the sergeant and all other noise but a dog barking at the waves. The boys watch in silence.

149

A GREAT many people know that Swansea is a Welsh seaport and manufacturing town, the centre of a district where it has been said that 'nine-tenths of the entire make of copper in Great Britain' is smelted; that it has claims to be called the 'Metropolis of South Wales'; that its football team beat the South Africans; that Beau Nash was born there, and Landor dwelt there, making love to some one named Ione or Jones, and writing 'Gebir'; that it possesses a ruined castle and a new 'Empire'; that it lies across the visitor's road to Gower. Here and there more can be heard of it. One of its parks, says a lady, had for some time a clock with the hours (like Marvell's dial) marked in flowers. Another avers that the town smells, and that the inhabitants either do not know or do not care, some holding the opinion that one of the smells is beneficial. — It is a magnificent town, of which some, if not Landor, might say even to-day that for scenery and climate it excels the Gulf of Salerno or the Bay of Naples. — It is a sordid hag of a town, sitting shameless amid the ruins of its natural magnificence. — It is as good as Blackpool. — There is 'nothing particular' in it, nothing old and picturesque, nothing new and grand or even expensive. — Many of its dark-

151

haired and pale-skinned women are beautiful. –
And so on.

But this I cannot understand: that some people
should be – and some are – indifferent to Swansea.
Year after year I go there (I do not mean to the
Mumbles, but to the town, and nothing but the
town), and walk up and down it and round about,
inhaling sea air and mountain air, or the smells
from copper works, cobalt works, manure works,
and fried-fish shops; year after year I have felt that
only friends could bring me again to Swansea.
But the town is a dirty witch. You must hate or
love her, and I both love her and hate her, and
return to her as often as four times in a year. It
is not this or that beautiful or hideous thing that
draws me. I do not go to see a woman pitching
broken crockery out of her front door into a street
where children go barefooted; nor to smell the
stale fat of the skin-yard, and see shaggy cattle
driven into the slaughter-house, and a woman
carrying a baby in a shawl after them; nor to
hear midnight quarrelling in the Irish quarter –
a woman at first having it her own way, shouting
louder and louder and drowning the man's bass
interjections, then wildly screaming 'Bastard, bastard,' until the cry is smothered in noises of scuff-
ling and throttling, and the victor's voice rising

for a moment as he strikes, and, after that, her sobbing and moaning, that ends in silence broken only by the child they have awakened. I do not go because they will tell me those brand-new edifices are on the site of the old block-cottages 'where the bad women lived' – as if the 'bad women' were used in the foundations or had been scared out of their iniquity by the splendours of architecture. The pleasant accidents are many in Swansea. The docks are always pleasant with the smell of tar, the weaving whirl of sea-gulls, the still ships, the cold green water reflecting the gaudy figurehead of the *Kate*, the men unloading potatoes, the painter slung under the bowsprit, with a fag in his mouth, which he puts behind his ear to whistle 'Away to Rio.' For that minute the ship looks like a beautiful great captive beast, beautiful in the same manner as the neighbouring caged thrush's song of pure thickets, the sun, the wind, and the rain. I like, too, the rag-and-bone man blowing one deep note on his horn as he travels mean streets; and the cockle-women (their white, scoured cockle-tubs on their heads or under their arms) from Penclawdd, dressed in half a dozen thicknesses of flannel, striped and checked, all different and all showy – with broad hips, no waists, stout legs slowly and powerfully moving, and the clearest of complexions and brightest of lips and eyes under their fine soft brown hair. Six days of the week I like the whole Swansea crowd of factory men and girls, the shawled mothers, the seamen, the country folk, though not one element is exceptionally picturesque.

These pleasant and unpleasant things, however, have little to do with the final effect, composite but very definite, of the whole town: they colour certain days, but no more. What counts most is the careless, graceless nature of Swansea, its lordly assemblage of chimney-stacks, its position at a river mouth between mountains, and the neighbourhood of the sea. Cheapness, *clapham-junction*, squalor, or actual hideousness is everywhere in contrast with grandeur, and even sublimity, and these qualities do not alternate, but conflict, or in some way co-operate. In the central streets, broad and glassy, thronged to the point of tumult with men and beasts and every kind of vehicle; in the outward-going roads of monotonous, and dismal or unclean, cottages, threaded by electric trams and country carts, and in sunless courts where privacy and publicity are one, you have always in sight either sea or mountain.

For the greater part of the town is built on riverside and seaside ground, where the mountains open a little wider apart to make way for the River Tawe. Two steep and treeless mountains hang over it. One of them, called at different points Mount Pleasant (where the workhouse is), Gibbet Hill, and Town Hill, is more or less green, but carved by quarries, and now higher and higher up striped with horizontal lines of plainest cottages and of villas pretending to some form of prettiness, all set among wastes of poor grass, feverfew, and wormwood. The straight ascents are as steep as the street at Clovelly, the paving-stones in some being tilted out of the flush to give a foot-hold. Once the springs in this hillside fed several wells of some fame, such as the Baptist Well and St. Helen's Well, which are commemorated only in the names of streets. Kilvey, the other hill, is green to seaward, but where it falls most abruptly, and the valley between it and the Town Hill is narrowest, it has been stripped by poisonous smoke and covered with a deposit of slag, except on the perpendicular juts, which reveal the strata of blackish rock; a chimney pierces the summit and stands out against the sky. The lowest parts alone of this hill are littered with houses, but on a high green terrace seaward linger a white rustic cottage and a small farm-house or two, and above them, at the very ridge, an old windmill tower.

The town cannot forget these two hills, whether they rise clear in their green or their drabby black, or whether the flurries of mist reveal a momentary and fragmentary glimpse of Kilvey's hilltop chimney or windmill tower, a grisly baseless precipice and a gull passing it, a gleam of white wall. Between the hills bends the river, the yellow Tawe. The factories crowd to its right bank, opposite to Kilvey, in order to get rid of their gilded and other filth, and to receive the ships; in the mud and yellow stones rests the two-masted *Audacieuse*, of St. Valery-sur-Somme, discharging phosphates, while three men in blue stand below to caulk and paint her. In spite of the colour of the water, numbers of people have fallen into it, some by accident, some after deliberation. The one foot-bridge crosses at the docks, where the character of the river is lost. Only a ferry plies from among the factories to the few undesirable houses under the steepest and barest part of Kilvey. A man, therefore, might live in Swansea without knowing of the river. But the mountains which it cleaves are omnipresent, and from many places its course can be seen far away inland through heights green with grass, grey with bare rock, or violet with distance.

The low waterside crowd of copper, steel, tin,

zinc, silver, cobalt, manure, and other works is the real Swansea. The remainder, the miles of flat-faced cottages here or upon the hill, is but an inexpensive prison where the workers may feed, smoke, read the newspapers, breed, and sleep. Those works vomit the smokes which Swansea people either ignore or praise; for when the smell from the manure works pervades the town, they expect fine weather from a north or north-east wind. They take you up on the Town Hill at night to see the furnaces in the pit of the town blazing scarlet, and the parallel and crossing lines of lamps, which seem, like the stars, to be decoration. If it is always a city of dreadful day, it is for the moment and at that distance a city of wondrous night. I have seen the steel works — I think when the roof was uncovered for repairs — look like a range of burning organ-pipes, while overhead hung, or imperceptibly flowed, a white spread of smoke, hiding the hills and half of the black, starry sky, but only half veiling the tall chimneys which silently increased it. At dawn it is worth while to see the furnaces paling, Kilvey very clear and dark, and the few stars white above it. Dawn climbs over Kilvey Hill into Swansea.

By day the scene is better, because the variety is greater, according to the wind and the lie of the sea mist, the river mist, and the smoke, both the accumulations and the individual tributaries of smoke; and because then can be seen the dim ridges of the greater mountains beyond the chimneys, and in the other direction a hundred moods of the sea and the coast hills. The furnaces, the vast, sooty sheds clanging and clattering, the fuming slag hills, where women crawl raking for something less than gold, and, above all, the grouped or single chimneys standing irregularly beside the river, are more worth looking at than a model town. As for the chimneys, like gigantic tree-trunks or temple pillars that have survived some gigantic desolation, these and their plumes of smoke or of flame are among the most unforgettable things that men have made. The black hills and vales of Landore, its fire-palaces and hundred smoke-stacks, compose one of the sublimest of all absolutely human landscapes. The slag heaps are venerable even in age. One of them, still growing in the midst of the town, is about a century old, and with the two blackened cottages nestling at its foot it would seem a considerable hill were it not backed and dwarfed by Kilvey. It is one of the boundaries to a characteristic Swansea waste – several uneven acres, strewn with brickbats, trodden in all directions, without grass, and on the other sides bounded by houses, a big school, and a church about as high as the hill of slag. Evidently this land once served some purpose, is now disused, and is waiting for a day when time is no longer money. Similar spaces are sometimes occupied by the town refuse, which the east wind distributes and the 'Rising Sun' washes down. Out of one broad space, black and scarred by watercourses from the mountain, a small part has been railed in for a children's playground, with swings, parallel bars, and seats; but no grass grows there. Numerous lesser wastes mark where houses have been or are to be, and at present they are useful sites for a pile of tins, glass, earthenware, rags, sweepings, tea-leaves, and fish-bones; nettle and wormwood flourish. These are in the more domestic portions of the town. Among the factories can be seen many a disastrous black wilderness, a black, empty amphitheatre traversed by the yellow river. Another kind of waste is the marshland above the town proper, invaded on one side by tips of slag, but too marshy for the most cynical builder, and still left, therefore, to rush and thistle.

Everywhere decay and ruin make their boast side by side with growth. Disused workshops are not supplanted, but are spared by some form of piety to stand and thin into skeletons, with gaping walls and roofs, to fall gradually in heaps among their successors. The sheds with rafters broken, tiles slipping, bricks dislodged, the derelict and tumbling cottages, the waste places of slag, old masonry, and dust, tufted with feverfew, the yards cumbered by rusty iron implements and rubbish, the red rivulet plunging in black gorges, speak rather of a bloodily conquered and deserted city than of a claimant to be the 'Metropolis of South Wales.' But round the corner a new block of buildings, including a chemist's and a sweet-shop, followed by cottages with painted wooden porches, and then a three-year-old chapel filled by a noble hymn wailing triumphantly, and next a view of twenty chimneys and of hills divided into squares of corn and grass and irregular woods, revive the claim. And yet this chapel is at the foot of a rough quarried slope sprinkled thinly and anyhow with white and whitish cottages among rushes and tufted grass, which is a scene of an almost moorland sweetness for those living in the new-old streets of eternal smoke under the mountain opposite, barren and black.

The same piety spares also the deserted dwelling. The old mountain farm-house, whose pastures entertain footballers instead of cattle, is left to gather moss and docks on its thatch, and stones (thrown at the windows) in all its rooms. The ferry-boat from the works over to Foxhole, a straggling settlement between the bare steep of Kilvey Hill and the river, lands you by a bunch of four old cottages of the colour of scorched paper, the walls of their tiny yards collapsing, and all windowless except the one which gives some reason for supposing it to be inhabited by human beings. Nearer the centre of the town other dwellings have attained a similar condition. Whole streets of houses, too old at fifty or sixty, have been condemned, but are still used because they are, at any rate, warmer than the outer air. When new cottages are built they often stand against the ruined ones instead of taking their places, just as the new church at Llansamlet stands against the partly ruinous old tower.

The houses are seldom of the material and make to be comely in their old age. The flat fronts shed their grimy plaster in flakes; the windows are like the eyes of the blind; the miniature gardens consist of fowl-houses, nasturtiums, and cats; and from the gramophone comes a frivolous London tune, or from the harmonium 'Yes, Jesus loves me,' while at the back door a woman washes in the sun. Until they are well advanced in decay, they are hardly interesting, save to the occupiers and to sanitary authorities and housing committees. Almost all of them have been erected in long, straight bars or blocks during the early or late nineteenth century. They peel or split and become dirty, but their two windows and a door, or three windows and a door, have to depend for variety of expression on a barber's pole or coloured advertisements; very few have front gardens. Old age and neatness seldom adorn the same house in Swansea. As it ages it falls into worse and worse hands; the garden is given over to wormwood, and a piece of semi-rustic slum is completed. Signs of ease, opulence and pleasure, mysteriously created by men and machinery, are to be seen in the high-placed villas towards the sea, but they have no individuality except what is given here and there by a piece of cliffy garden.

The best, as well as probably the oldest, building in Swansea is the castle. It is wedged in, and actually incorporated, among shops and dwellings, though it displays a beautiful range of arcading above their roofs; a telegraph-post sticks up in the middle; but it still protects a small, inaccessible patch of long green grass on one side between it and the street wall, where a building site is advertised. Its position low down near the river, ob-

scured by the glories of the principal street, denies
it the impressiveness of the so-called Trewyddfa
Castle which crowns a steep isolated hill farther
inland at the verge of the town. This is a spare,
craggy ruin, like a few rotten old teeth, near Landore station, but high and distinct above the pale,
scrambling cottages of the slopes. Not a hundred
years ago, they say, the 'castle' was built by a
public man as a residence, that he might refute
with ostentation the charge of penury. But he was
not a Norman baron, and, lacking power or courage or imagination to raid the neighbourhood with
arms, he could not endure life on his eminence
very long. The forsaken mansion was let out in
tenements, failed as such, and was finally offered
to rain and wind as the material for an apparently
feudal ruin. They have performed their task to
admiration: Trewyddfa Castle is the only thing in
Swansea to satisfy a taste for the mediæval picturesque. At the foot of its hill, horses pasture among
gipsy vans, slag heaps, cottages, and the remains of
cottages.

Swansea is too busy to invent an Arthurian or
feudal tale about this 'castle,' or in any way to coin
money out of it. Of the vanity of picturesqueness
the town altogether lacks traces. And yet some
money has been spent on making the old round

windmill tower, towards the seaward and green
end of Kilvey Hill, impervious to weather, boys,
and the few dirty-faced cows of those pastures.
Seats have been placed on two sides, because it is
on the flat at the very top of the hill, and eastward, southward and northward the eye ranges
without impediment. To the south are the lowest-
lying parts of Swansea, the mathematical lines of
the docks, a steamer hooting as she enters, many
sailing vessels at rest and silent, and trains shunt-
ing with noises as of a drunken orchestra tuning
up – the yellow-sanded bay curving under a wall
of woods to the horned rocks and lighthouse of
the Mumbles – the main sea and the aerial distant
masses of Exmoor and the Mendips. A world of
domed or abrupt mountains to the north is broken
up by the valleys of the Neath and Tawe rivers.
The waveless, effervescent blue sea to eastward is
edged by dunes, and behind them by wooded or
bracken-covered high hills with emerald clefts;
and the white and the dirty smoke of Neath and
Port Talbot rises between the sands and the hills.

The seats round the windmill tower are a little
worn, but I never saw anyone there, nor met anyone who had been there. Why should people go
up? Not to gain a view, certainly. Swansea has as
many views as smells. Every street has a view at

SWANSEA VILLAGE

one end or the other; some have one at both. For
example, Byron Crescent, and, better still, Shelley
Crescent, new streets high up on the green hill and
curving with it, command so much of sea and
mountain that their names are not ridiculous.
Steepness forbids houses to be built on both sides
of the horizontal street, and enables Shelley
Crescent to look clear over the back of Byron
Crescent. One end looks on Kilvey Hill, the
riverside works at its foot, the lines of the multitudes of cottages, the dotted 'castle' mound, and
beyond it the greater mountains. The scene from
the other end includes first the docks, the slated,
rectangular labyrinth of the town, hardly diversi-
fied by a few churches, a gasometer, and here and
there a row of elms or poplars, or a single tree,
projecting as it were out of fissures in that mass of
brick and stone; and then the silver, cold, rippled
sea, with slashes of foam, stretching away to the
hills of Glamorgan, hazy with smoke, and to the
hills of Somerset, which are as clouds. In twenty
years Shelley Crescent will be old, and they will
have forgotten to paint the woodwork; but the sea
and the far mountains will be the same, and Kilvey
can hardly avoid being still half green, half black.
By that time Swansea may have a quarter of a
million inhabitants; I shall not guess whether the

village will have become a town. At present it is probably more a village than when the borough counted about a thousand under Elizabeth. Its activity in spreading hither and thither has kept it from thinking about anything but factories, docks, and the necessities of life. That is the dark charm of Swansea to one who has not to live in it. It is careless of itself, of its majestic position, its lovely neighbourhood, its hundred and twenty thousand men, women, and children. Compared with Cardiff, it is a slattern. Yet, being a spectator, I am glad that I have known Swansea between these hills, and not a lesser Cardiff or Liverpool. Equally shameless and unpretentious, it swarms about the Tawe, climbs over the hill with inconsiderate vitality, always allowing the magnitude and precipitousness of its hills to have full effect, while they in their turn emphasize the rustic squalor and confused simplicity of the town, combining with it to make a character which at the same moment irritates and fascinates.

GLAMORGAN

THE man who knows Glamorgan knows Wales. It is a land of mountains much divided by rivers and rivulets, increasing in height and wildness inland, but having between the mountains and the sea a fertile border which varies from a few hundred yards to several miles in breadth. This fertile land is decorated by the large number of castles which once protected the Normans against the mountain Welshmen. The rivers supply large and numerous steel works, copper works, tinplate works, etc., and receive from them poison of many colours. The mountains are pierced by coal-mines and carved by quarries. Glamorgan possesses the great manufacturing towns and seaports of Cardiff and Swansea, the cathedral of Llandaff, the ancient townlet of Lantwit, and countless ruins, such as Neath Abbey, and the castles of Caerphilly, Coity, Kenfig, and Oystermouth. Some of its valleys, like those of Rhondda and Maesteg, are of the blackest; others, like that of Neath, are among the greenest; those of the Twrch and Mellte are very wild. It includes Llanmaes, one of the quietest places under the sun, as well as Dowlais and Tonypandy; and the large peninsula of Gower is shared between visitors and agriculture, though at the very edge of it stands Landore, where men

167

have toiled for centuries to show what a town is when it is nothing but a town, where earth and air and river are chiefly dirt. It has yellow rivers like the Tawe, and rivers like the Perddin, the Camffrd and the Thaw, which are as living crystal where they are not white as milk. The coast is one of precipices, as throughout half of Gower; of sand-hills, as at Porthcawl. It is a land of mines, of furnaces, and slums, but also of the richest and gentlest fields, as in the Vale of Glamorgan, still gleaming with the white houses which were praised hundreds of years ago by poets. And, east and west, there is hardly a hill-top but commands the sea.

Other counties have a similar variety of characters, but Glamorgan shows them altogether in a hundred places. From the windmill tower above Swansea, for example, you see the ships and the chimneys of Swansea, Neath, and Port Talbot; but you see also, on the one hand, corn, pasture, moorland, and white cottages, the rivers Neath and Tawe cleaving with their romantic valleys a great realm of mountains; on the other hand, the blue waters and yellow sands of a sea that extends thirty miles away southward to Exmoor. The same, or as much, can be commanded from the neighbour-hood of Cardiff, Pontypridd, Neath, or Pontar-

dulais. A composite portrait of the county would
show green fields, black fields, a hundred chimneys
pouring out fire and smoke, a white farm-house
with its sheds and lodges shining like a negro's
teeth, and a background of mountains with
cataracts among their crags and fern. But composite portraits are without life. To combine, for
example, the Vale of Glamorgan with Morriston,
Landore, and Swansea is like mixing an apple with
a lump of coal, which would make neither food nor
fuel. And yet you have often equally great con-
trasts side by side, especially during the first stages
in the growth of a place like Pontardulais – when
it is being transformed from a village with a
fulling-mill and an inn to a Hell, fully equipped.
Then the purest green fields border on the factory
yard, and will be ready to encroach on it if deserted.
The old white cottage of Glamorgan will stand side
by side with the cheapest town type, in which the
mortar is made with sand instead of coal. Where
there used to be a live otter is now a dead dog or
two. By the little solitary farm under the four
sycamores the miner greets the shepherd, and the
mountain sheep and their lambs, which are prettier
than deer, feed close to the smoke, provided that
the west wind carries it off the pasture, not on
to it. These things are to be found every year

169

by anyone who walks twenty or thirty miles in
Glamorgan.

In the course of such a walk you see every
variety. In the morning you are in a green castle
court which Owen Glendower visited; a horse
grazes among the tall fragments of masonry,
draped with ivy, felted with grass and daisy,
tufted with little ash trees, and the blue of two
peacocks nodding across burns in the sunshine. A
robin sings, the rooks caw on their way to the
stubble, the jackdaws chaff one another in the clear
sky above their woods. In the south lies the sea,
in the north the mountains; and the earth is as
tranquil as the sky. You pass nothing worse all
the morning than a quarry and golf-links. At midday you have on your left the sand-dunes, on your
right the mountains, to which the trees, yellow and
red and bare, are fitted like a bird's breast-feathers.
The curlews cry over the road as you approach
factories and ships, and a town of mean streets
and enormous 'pubs,' of bustle, prosperity, and
pale faces. Before evening you are in a valley of
chimneys, skirting a wide, barren marsh, where
black streamlets run, and women search for something on the slopes of fuming slag-mountains.
Gradually, the turns of the valley reveal, first, a
hundred tall stacks and their attendant fleeces of

smoke, white, black, or tawny, and then a hundred masts and funnels, a crescent of yellow sand, the blue water of Swansea Bay, with the Mumbles lighthouse to the right, and to the left the horizontal white band of cottages on the red mountain above Port Talbot, three miles away. In many other directions a similar walk may be taken. The mountainous pit alone in which Swansea lies will furnish, on a lesser scale, the same contrasting and yet combining elements of grace, majesty, and horror, of blue sea and green hill, of coal-mine, copper works, and slums. The town and its coast and hills make as accurately as possible a composite portrait of Glamorgan. But then it is also possible to spend a whole day within the county and never quit the fern, heather, and whinberry of the stony mountains; and another day in exuberant undulating country as sweet as Kent, but bounded by mountains; and yet another without any variety except in the smoke you breathe, the ashes you tread, the colour of the streams and the number of the pit-mouths or chimneys in sight. To see it all is to see Wales – I do not say to know it.

WHEN three or four races had been run, the crowd of poorer and of non-sporting on-lookers spread once more over the course, but as few pretty women and gay dresses remained in the select enclosures, the crowd turned away, and the course became almost empty. Some lay on the slopes below and ate or smoked; below them small bands of early-goers and late-comers were mounting or descending the paths of the hillsides. Beyond them, and above the tree-hidden village and railway station, the land rose again into many rounds of bald or beech-capped hill, and beyond these into a level ridge that was all one oak wood. Here the barley was in stooks; there the oats were obliterated by poppies. Under one dark edge of beechwood a broad field was lemon-coloured with charlock. Above all was a cloudy and windy sky, now and then permitting gleams out of the blue to give a summer sound to the broil of continually tossing branches in the beechwoods of the hills, and the elm clusters by farm and wayside.

The earth, like the sky, seemed to have nothing to do with the flimsy white grandstand on the hill-top, the long white rails lining the curved course, and the gay crowd and the grey crowd. The only difference to the earth was that the grass and furze of the near slopes were decked abundantly with paper of several hues, and that the paths of the neighbourhood were trampled into mire and extended to the width of a wide road.

The greater numbers of both crowds were on the other side of the course, where drink, food, betting and amusements were to be had, with a dark background of stately and innumerable beeches, the 'birdless woods.' There were long rows of motor-cars, carts, and bookmakers' stands; behind them a row of booths for eating and drinking and games of some skill and more luck; and behind these again the caravans and low tents of the gipsies and other nomads; then the road and the high wall of the 'birdless woods,' noisy with the wind and yet looking silent.

Now in the interval the bookmaker, 'Joe' or 'Charlie,' could heave his vast bulk out of the cart and arrive somehow upright upon the ground below with garments still unburst by the quaking volume of flesh which they contained. In solitude, but not in silence, he licked up two plates of salmon with much vinegar. Now the dark sportsman, with frowning face, bulging eyes, and square blue jaws, stood munching bread and lobster, converting it, with even more determination than content, into frowning face, bulging eyes, and square

174

blue jaws. Some one had given oranges to the bare-legged band who had been tumbling about, swearing, cheerfully quarrelling and backing the jockey with the red cap and black shirt, etc., and they ate the peel whilst watching the lobster-eater without too much envy. He in his turn had half an eye upon a gipsy woman of enormous bulk. She was certainly as much a 'sitting' as a 'religious' or 'laughing' animal. She sat alone, among the horses, in a deep yellow blouse, many-coloured gaudy shawl, black skirt, and high-feathered black hat. Without stirring anything but an eye, she watched the young bony-faced women from neighbouring tents – their brown faces newly washed, their black hair combed and evenly parted, their eyes bright as with a little quicksilver, and their lips smiling, as they bent down, holding buckets at a pump worked by the menfolk.

The spectators flowed in streams and masses alongside the tents of the gipsies, who were washing, cooking, eating, talking, or educating the young, exactly as if they were surrounded, not by a crowd, but by four walls of a house. Their horses were not more unconcerned, though they were more still, with patient bended necks. Stillest of all were the hounds, curled up, and silent and asleep, all but their eyes and ears. Sometimes the

crowd formed an island to allow two knowing
little barefooted boys to box, or a ponderous, ill-
featured couple to dance, all beaming with alcohol
and mutual affection. The gipsies and other show-
men were blessed with strange contentment. For
example, at the end of the row of stalls and
coconut-shies a man was standing in charge of a
great low table. Clients were to spin the indicator
and thus just possibly win one of the coconuts or
plates of shell-fish upon the table. He was a burly
man, as broad as he was long, with a face like
leather, and stiff black hair and moustache, and no
roof to his mouth. He invited clients by a powerful monotonous cry of 'Come along. You can't
all win. You can't all win'—which was a very
accurate statement. As he ended the cry he
stooped, and with great ease won a plate of shell-
fish. This he refused to eat, having won it only to
encourage others. He then repeated his cry of
'Come along. You can't all win. You can't all
win.' Powerful as was his voice, his deformity
made him almost unintelligible, and for this or
some other reason – as, for example, the philosophic accuracy of his thought, if not his speech
– no one answered his call. Yet he also had
this strange content, and obviously no fear of
to-morrow, death, or anything else. He was no

ghost. But the crowd was ghostly. The nomads, working and idling, were real enough, but not so the main crowd, eating, drinking, smoking, betting, or looking on. It was a childless crowd, and there were few women. Laughter was not infrequent, but no smiles could be seen. The visitors were not at ease: collected from everywhere, and massed together, they had yet nothing in common but internal solitude and external pursuit of pleasure. Separated from their homes in Lambeth, Redhill, or Portsmouth, they seemed to have lost their identity. Their immortal souls had taken holiday, scattered about perchance like the paper on the gorse of the hillside. They were nothing but bodies, dark suits and bowler hats. The man with no roof to his mouth was not a ghost, but I can make no such assertion about any of the multitude, of which I was one.

The most native and natural to the place of all these thousands were the four white 'minstrels' and one blacked bone-man, who appeared in this interval for the first time. The white duck suits (with purple collars and cuffs) and straw hats seemed a kind of undress in which they had been surprised; and they matched the trivial white grandstand and temporary buildings, and might have been born and brought up there. The sight

of them made me think of the summery white
woodwork in December, and the minstrels en-
camped in it alone amidst the wind, rain and frost
of the high solitary downs. Even on that day,
whenever the sun was in the cloud, the wind was
chill. It was chill as the minstrels came out, wip-
ing their lips from the meanest of the refreshment
booths. None of them was young, and none was
fat. Two had not dyed their grey hair. All were
clean-shaven and had regular features, colourless,
hard actor faces and grey eyes. The eldest, a
venerable sharp-faced boy of fifty, was limping.
They remained silent and in single file as they put
away the ends of their cigarettes, and climbed the
steep bank up to the course, stooped in a brisk-
looking style under the rails, and crossed over to a
place within two yards of an enclosure. There
they formed a line, still in silence; but after a brief
glance at one another they plucked their banjos
while the bone-man grinned a flashing grin, shak-
ing his black college cap, so that the red tassel
fell towards his nose.

Suddenly they began to play and sing. As they
did so, even the venerable 'father' of the company
began also to sway and rise and fall from heel to
toe with a jauntiness to match the tune. The few
men and women still strolling in the enclosure

now strolled vaguely towards the minstrels, and one or two even stopped by the iron railings and stared at them in silence. One beautiful, fair, tall woman, of not quite forty, the only woman in the enclosure, and her daughter of about eleven, both in white and green, came up and watched them smilingly, her head thrown in a sort of kindly haughtiness back under her yellow parasol. Others came and went, but these two stayed. They smiled out of perfect health and good nature, but partly also in pity for the singers, and in scornful amusement at the song.

The four minstrels, known among themselves and to some seaside crowds as 'The Bonny Bachelors,' were singing the joys of watering-places, of summer holidays spent in drinking copiously and walking out with 'lots of girls.' The five verses brought before the mind this vision. A crescent of tall, gaunt boarding-houses and hotels following the line of a bay from an old castle at one end to an abrupt cliff at the other. Half-way between the castle and cliff a pier, painted white, and running far out into the sea on countless long thin legs. A promenade, the whole length of the crescent, having a stone parapet and a wide stone pavement continuously trodden by holiday-makers. Here and there two or three young men

dawdle up and down with light canes and cigarettes, and make eyes at bunches of girls slightly
below them in class. Out at the pier end a band
plays jerky, frivolous music. A few sails dot the
bay. A white motor-boat throbs fussily out to sea.
On the green rocks below the castle end of the
parapet a lonely man is casting a fishing-line far
into the still water. The sea is clear blue in the hot,
perfect weather. With the aid of brandy and soda-
water – of some blearing of the eyes and much dull
spending of the spirit of youth – the glare of the
sun and the blue sky, the long dim outline of the
high coast, the glittering sea, the heather and sea
air, and the loud music, the glances, neat forms
and happy movements of girls, mingle in the
minds of the young men into a half-delirious and
half-dreamy hope, so that they seem to be walking
in a world like that of a musical opera, of wicked-
ness, gay, expensive and without ending, where all
the women were as beautiful as that one in the
enclosure at Goodwood, and all the old men as
frivolous as the grey-haired minstrel.

The song had a jaunty tune, composed, as it
was meant to be sung and heard, in a state of in-
complete intoxication. It combined languor and
jauntiness to a miracle. It was continually tending
to perish of languor and continually rescued by

jauntiness. It expressed, with a perfect under-standing of popular opinion, the gaiety of bachelors and emancipated husbands.

The beautiful fair lady and her pretty daughter stood and smiled at the middle-aged minstrels singing the dull, saucy chorus again and again. The happiness and beauty of these two in the light of the sun was so full that everything partook of them. If they heard the skylarks singing above the birdless woods they did not discriminate be-tween that music and this of the 'Bonny Bache-lors.' Each gave them an equal opportunity for happiness, and a fresh excuse for a smile.

The fifth verse was sung with all the determina-tion of the first, and the toes of the most aged minstrel seemed not to tire of rising and falling to the tune. While the chorus was still being re-peated the blacked bone-man took off his college cap and made as if to ask the listeners for rewards. Immediately, all within the enclosure, except the mother and daughter, gave some more or less consummate intimation of having just then some-thing else to do, and they stalked off as slowly as was compatible with safety before their charity was undeniably besought. The beautiful lady did not move away, but even came a little nearer, right to the railings, and smiled and said a few words which gave her happiness, while she and her daughter put something into the college cap. Everyone else on the course as well as in the enclosure had escaped the appeal. Nevertheless, after an interval spent in silence while the bone-man was away, up again went the purple cuffs to the banjos, and up went the heels of the cricket shoes, and the tune was repeated. Still the lady smiled, either at the minstrels or at her daughter. Only after the third verse, and without any sign of weariness, but smiling and gently giving a bow, which the bone-man returned with prodigious courtesy, she moved away with the sunshine. The crowd was now thick about them, and there were too many coming and going for the bone-man to fill his cap; those that stood still were looking at the beautiful two departing, not at the minstrels. They made an end only just in time to leave the course with the crowd before the next race. In slow, silent procession, still looking the only natives, the soiled white and purple and the mis-fitting black of the 'Bonny Bachelors' were distributed in the crowd, to re-light their half-cigarettes, to watch the moment's inhuman fury and beauty of the horses passing in the race, and, when it was over, to return and hope to see their patronesses again. When the eldest of them appeared to be about to consult a bookmaker, some one in the crowd flung the jeer: 'Think of your wife and family'; but he joined in silence as before the jauntily bobbing row of the 'Bonny Bachelors' playing the old tune.

Just above where the cattle have trampled the steep bank into a gently sloping morass, a low bridge crosses the stream, a bridge of oak boughs covered so with soil that it seems part of the field. For the most part the stream is lined on both sides by alders, but at the bridge, above the drinking-place, there are three beech trees. They appear to have begun to grow out horizontally over the water and then to have made an effort by which they rose sixty feet straight into the air; at the curve where this change took place the boles are very broad and corrugated with protuberances like pectoral muscles, and one of them might well have been modelled in dark stone from a giant's breast astrain. The stream has worn away the banks far under the roots, which are knotted into a grey lattice-work where the moorhen and watervole retreat and where many a child has gained its first image of a cave. The stream itself is crystal in substance and, being deeply sunk, is never ruffled by wind; lower down it is broken by stepping-stones, but here it is pure and polished, and it is streaked and bestarred by waving green strands and leaves of water-plants which add the tenderness of vegetation to the severity of the cold depths and glooms and flashes of the water.

185

Below the bridge the white and strawberry cows drink and wade between the high banks, and then stand and lazily raise their knees above the surface at long intervals and crop the leaves that brush their horns.

Above the bridge there is a break in the dense herbage of meadow-sweet and sweet-foliaged tansy opposite the beeches. The bank is lower there and it is possible to sip the rapid water. As you lie down and stretch your head from the bank, the trout, hardly distinguishable from the clear element except by his spots, darts away over the ruddy and amber stones. Your image trembles in the mirror and dies away like a dream on the border of sleep. You hear the cool, pure, busy voice of single purpose and joy. For an instant the physical nearness seems about to discover a spiritual affinity between your soul and the crystal shade into which you plunge your face. The water washes away more than the sadness and dullness from the eyes, more than the thirst from the lips, and the white, the gold, or the violet blossoms on the bank gleam to the sight as if it were emparadised. You rise, unchanged, indeed, but having caught, and perhaps lost again, a faint sense of the old reverence for springs and running water, remembering how the shepherd Aristæus, son of

186

Apollo and of Cyrene, the nymph of a holy foun-
tain, went to the brink of his mother's river in his
great need and called to her, and descended into
the flood down to her cold caverns, and gained
from her an ambrosial fragrance, wisdom and
great strength; remembering the words of the
wise Greek poet, bidding men not to cross a river
before they have prayed with eyes turned to the
source and have washed their hands in the fair
pale water, lest the gods be angry and give them
grief; and how the never sorrowful Muses, having
bathed in Hippocrene or the violet spring on
Helicon, danced lightly upon the holy and lofty
mountain, and went forth and sang of the gods
with their sweet voices and taught the poets.

There is no fairer brook than this, winding with
its alders through the plain of grass, from which
the land rises in round undulations to the woods
and precipitous chalk hills of the near horizon,
where the spring buds forth under the beeches.
The plain is worthy of any concourse of beauty or
nobleness of which history or poetry or legend
tells. Large and level enough for a jousting, it
covers itself most naturally to the fancy – when the
sunlight is very splendid upon the grass and the
three beeches and the high beechwoods beyond –
with Arthurian pavilions, white and gold and blue,

and shields hanging at the doors, and horses
pasturing and young knights playing their fierce
games: or the eye sees it deserted save for one
figure, seated by the flashing stream under the
beeches, that of the mad naked knight Sir Tris-
tram of Liones harping to himself and weeping
over the melody of the harp and the memory of
Beale Isoud and of her loveliness; or that of Sir
Launcelot du Lake, after the death of Elaine,
when he went daily 'to a well fast by the hermitage,
and there he would lie down, and see the well
spring and bubble, and sometimes he slept there.'

But here in fact the children drink, and then
paddle and splash and walk far down the stream.

Here comes, fresh from prison, on some May
day the tall grey fool who spends one-half of his
life in picking wild flowers and ferns, snaring
rabbits, haymaking, fruit-picking, chopping up
wood, and digging for ladies who have gardens
on a light soil; the other half in prison. He is one
of those men whom every one smiles at and instinctively calls 'Jack.' The sight of such a one
puts every one in a good humour, partly because
he is himself always smiling or ready to smile, and
partly because there is no one so poor or unfortunate or old as not to feel himself after the first glance
superior to or better off in some way than this

tatterdemalion. He has lost his taste for water, but likes to drink here and then dip his head under the beeches; also there are three trout there who hover in order of seniority with heads up-stream under the opposite bank, and Jack likes to see how they are getting on.

But the most regular visitor is the white-haired, white-aproned woman who comes every day from the almshouse to fill her pail. Very slowly she walks across the meadow up to the gap in the tansy and meadow-sweet. It is a quarter of an hour's walk for her, but she spends half an hour over it because she stops and puts down her pail several times on the way. When she thus stands still she claps her hands under her apron and looks towards the apple-tree which stands near the site of the old mill. It is not at the apple-tree that she looks, though it is huge and gnarled and almost as green in winter as in summer by reason of the many bushes of mistletoe in its branches. She looks at the long splash of the water that no longer has any mill-wheel to turn, and at the green mounds which mark the foundations of the mill-house. On still nights she hears the dull thunder of the water when all those miles of woodland on the hills are dumb, and when they are all roaring she strives to disentangle that other noise. Child and woman

and crone, she has never dwelt out of hearing of
that falling water.

She was born in the house whose walls shook
with the turning of the vast green-bearded black
wheel that ground her father's flour and was her
first terror and delight. He was the miller, already
when she was a child a slow, stout man with a
white beard. His were several of the farms between the mill and the hills, and also on the high
land on the top of the hills, and he ground their
corn and grew rich; and not only rich but
fabulously so over half a county, and as she sat
watching, the wheel-men driving past would wave
their whips towards the dusty boarded mill and
the small brown house and say: 'No one knows
how rich Old Pile is; he was rich when I was a
boy and he never spends anything; he has never
done anything except grow rich.' They used to
say that the miller threw bags of gold into the
mill-pond on dark nights so that no one should
know his possessions, and that was why he would
never let any of the boys fish there, and why he
hung about all day when the squire was fishing,
apologetically but constantly. But Polly never saw
any of the gold.

Her mother was the pretty, sluttish, ever-busy
maidservant, the old man's slave, an orphan whom

he never allowed to go away for a day, for an hour.
He had promised her that she should inherit his
money, and proud at first to be thus favoured,
she held up her head and flouted the jeering and
insinuating; but she died at the birth of this child.

The old man reared Polly entirely by himself.
Born in servitude and ignominy, she would be
more completely subdued even than her mother
had been. There could be no escape for her. She
would be a possession like his gold, a little costlier
to keep, and not to be hidden under the waters of
the pond. 'Some day you will be richer than the
squire,' she remembered him saying, and it was
her earliest memory: it was said to ease the miller's
feelings and not to reach the brain of his child,
but there it stayed.

She grew up quietly afraid of the man who was
waiting impatiently for her to take her mother's
place as maid-of-all-work at all hours of day and
night. But if she was afraid of the old man, she
was terrified by others. He taught her to fear and
to hate, to fear and hate others, and finally himself.
The labourers were idlers, poachers, thieves; the
farmers were feeble, always trying to get the better
of him; the squire was a fool and living on his
forefathers because he had not the wit to waste
their money: in some way all were the miller's

énemies and therefore hers, since if she was a good girl and did as he wished she would be richer than the squire. More than she hated them – for she had her mother's tenderness – she feared them.

The old man was not unkind to her; he did not beat or starve her; but she was afraid of him because she never understood a word that he said to her as a child, and she knew that he never understood a word of hers, and because he had once wakened her in her bed and leaned over her in a terrible red nightcap she had never seen before and said: 'Be a good girl, better than your mother.' She was allowed to go to chapel with neighbours who passed the mill on their way. There she heard a chaos of dim wild things out of which emerged the image of some one, more grisly than her father, who might some day burst in upon her dreams with a voice of thunder, saying: 'Be a good girl.' It was terrible, and she hated the other people of her own accord when she saw how foolishly they relapsed into smiles and chatter as soon as they were outside the chapel. She was glad to be back at the mill, where it was easy to be good, to play with the cats and eat apples.

Once she climbed up into the old apple-tree, whence she could see two of her father's farms, many sheep and cattle, ploughs at work, the bright trees, the clouds stooping to them and seeming to be their brides, while nobody could see her. She stayed until nightfall, imagining her father dead, herself rich, and all the rest obedient or out of her sight, taught that they must not laugh outside the dark chapel and that unless they were good – she could not picture to herself among the clouds things cruel enough for a fit punishment. As the night blackened her father came to look for her, and suddenly she shouted, 'Old Pile' – for so she always heard him called and always thought of him – 'Old Pile, I am good.' He lifted her down, and showed so much satisfaction with this sign that the wish to please him was overcoming everything that she went happily to bed, and to dream that she was rich and had a hand-rail of gold up the steep hill, for herself alone.

She played with other children, haunted always by the love of good and the fear of the miller and of the deity. It was dark in the mill-house, and there were whole solitary days when it was the fascination of horror that kept her to the cavernous rooms and the old white-bearded man or god shuffling about in his huge slippers, or by the light of the fire – the perpetual fire on the broad hearth – reading *Pilgrim's Progress*. She played with a sense of theft and guilt, with a seriousness which

made her disliked by the other children and also
helped her to freaks and feats which they would
never have imagined. She frowned upon them at
their play because it was so careless and done
without thought of the terrible power dwelling
in the chapel, but not perfectly encaged there. She
herself was safe; she could please the miller, and
that was the whole of goodness: this gave her the
secret superiority to other children and the power
to triumph over their gay rebuffs. 'You are not
good,' she taunted them with a worldly religious
laugh, 'you will see.' In her father's sight she took
no notice of her playfellows. On sunny days she
often took a little stool and sat outside the open
front door, between the two low, dark-curtained
windows. The only garden was a strip not more
than a foot wide, running alongside the wall and
touching it, under these windows, and divided
from the road only by a broader sloping strip of
cobbles, polished brown. A fringe of 'snow-upon-
the-mountain' wandered a little from the garden
on to the cobbles; in their season there were snow-
drops, crocuses, wallflowers, sweet-rockets, and,
lastly, nasturtiums that also overflowed. Sometimes the cats curled up on these sunny stones and
frightened away the birds. Polly herself, seated
there on her stool, frightened away the children

who ventured for a moment to stay and talk and peer through the open door.

At every birthday she was very glad that she was getting old, because it brought her nearer. . . . She envied the big girls who were already as she desired to be, but despised them because they had had nothing to grow up for. Yet she was not impatient. The sense of power in Old Pile's house was immense. Nor when she began to perform many duties of the house was she conscious of any burden. Once, indeed, she was caught up to her middle in the pond, and feeling with her bare feet for the hidden gold; but even the miller's threats that if she did it again he would do something which was drowned and magnified in mutterings only added to her confidence in destiny.

To and fro she went from the mill to the nearest farm for milk, and by paths or along hedges over all the fields that were her father's and back to the mill, seeing the sun rise in the east and the southeast over his woods and set in the west and southwest behind the soft, large slopes of his pastures. A little maid, with black stiff hair, intensely shining black eyes that never changed; a little maid, a little life, and the knowledge that one day this land from sunrise to sunset would be her own.

She was not more than fifteen when he died in

his bed alone at night. She lay in her bed until midday, waiting for him to call her as he always did. She luxuriated in the sound of the church bells and the chapel-going children clattering as they rambled over the cobbles of the still house; she slept, woke, and slept again. When she was hungry she stole down and made herself tea, silently polished the brasswork in the kitchen and slipped out of the house. At her return she found a neighbour's wife at the house, who said, 'Old Pile is dead.' 'That's why he didn't want any breakfast,' said Polly, her hopes beginning to flutter, but not so much as to be irrepressible before an inferior. She slept in the same house as the corpse that night, disturbed only by a fear lest the soul should have taken away some of the cash (a thing that seemed possible to one who had seen £100 in the form of a sheet of paper such as even a common man's ghost might carry), and in the morning lit no fires because there was none to command her. The neighbour came again, and Polly, feeling helpless in the lone house and not having a halfpenny to buy the morning's milk, was not sorry to leave the mill. She was taken into service at the squire's house, where one of her old playfellows was a servant and gave an occasion for perpetuating her consciousness of superiority.

It was not before many months that she understood that others were for the time being, and had
been for some time past, enjoying what was hers
by right at the mill. 'Not yet,' she reflected; she
was used to waiting. She did her work poorly
because of her dream and her pride, and this
brought unfriendliness and blame, and these again
fostered her pride. She could wait. She smiled
inwardly in her sense of power. She consented to
walk out with the under-groom: it was pleasant to
be with men, for they flattered her, and that it
was because she was a maid did not occur to her:
but she would not entertain an offer of marriage
from the under-groom, who very likely knew her
fortune. Pride made her a bad servant but a good
manager of others, and it was as a tyrant that she
rose above them.

She kept her secret well; she sacrificed to it
her girlhood, she sacrificed her womanhood.
Dressed in dark clothes, with her white face and
those black eyes never changing, seeing without
noticing, her grey hands very still, she was a
breathing image that waited in pride and secrecy,
waited and did nothing else, except when, as house-
keeper, she snapped out commands which owed
their weight, as she sadly knew, to the squire's
position, not her own. It was only gradually, see-

ing at last that her grey hairs were many, that she
began to think she ought to make haste, and to
realize that alone she was powerless. But who
could help? All feared her, and she was solitary
as Old Pile and without a child — a stern, com-
petent, withered woman who saw clearly everything close at hand, everything of to-day and to-
morrow. There had been injustice. Her father
must have been mad: he had never made a will,
and so she was not yet the owner of his houses
and lands. His intention was beyond question;
only, she could not prove it. She had never mentioned it or her hope to anyone but the recipient
of her prayers. How, then, was it to be enforced?

The least unfriendly of the men and women
employed about the same house was the coachman.
He was younger than she, a man who had been
suddenly awakened by the death of a mother
whom he had kept for twenty years, and as yet
knew hardly what was to be done, but sat down
to wait apparently with content, certainly with
much tobacco. He was the groom who had
courted her thirty years ago. It came into her
head to take him into partnership in her hopes.
Suppose she married him . . . he would have a
good reason for helping her to the utmost to gain
her rights, and she respected his powers; he had

never done or spoken ill to her. Wilcocks, knowing her ability, certain that she had saved a pretty
sum, was not unwilling for such a coasting
venture. But when, on the return from church to
the cottage which was the squire's present, her
husband put his arm round her waist and said
genially, pointing to the garden, the tool-shed and
the newly painted white railings, 'Polly, my girl,
I am not sorry I waited these thirty years for you
and this little place,' then she thrust him away in a
rage of regrets and a fever of hopes, all the more
violent for her indignation that he should take a
liberty with the heiress of Old Pile. She thrust
him away and she told him the tale, concluding:
'You didn't know what you were marrying, Albert.
Two heads are better than one, or I should never
have married you. We must see that I get my
rights.'

The secret was now two people's. She used to
sit in the back doorway and watch him digging,
and say, 'Albert, it won't be for long,' and he
paused – for a moment only; he dared not rest
under her eye – to say, 'Just to think of you being
a rich woman all these years, Polly, at least by
right.' But Wilcocks' knowledge of the world
suggested nothing to him as he sauntered slowly
of a summer evening and leaned and looked at the

mill-wheel and took a rich glance at the house: he continued his walk and on the strength of his prospects drank whisky at 'The Good Intent' instead of ale. He asked Polly if they had not better compromise with the occupier of the mill and offer to take enough to keep a cow and buy a gramophone; but she merely asked what was a cow and a gramophone to her. At the inn Wilcocks nodded mysteriously and threw out vague hints, and once, on stepping out, went the length of refusing to touch his cap to the passing squire.

At last the time was approaching when it would be necessary to become possessed of his wife's fortune if the supply of whisky was to be kept equal to his demand. He made an effort just before this point was reached. This time his nods and hints were to his wife. He wanted a couple of pounds and it would be all right; it was to be a surprise for her birthday. A few days after, when she was just sixty-one, he took her for a walk in the early morning and showed her, here on a barn door, there on a wall, on a stile, on a beech at the wood's edge, on the side wall of the mill itself, the notice:

TRESPASSERS WILL BE PROSECUTED, BY ORDER
OF THE RIGHTFUL OWNER.

They came to the mill last of all and they went by in proud silence, not without anxiety. Day after day they waited for the result. Simmering with pride, they hardly cared to go outside the gate. They became conscious of something ridiculous in the fact that a revolution of this importance had been so quietly brought about by two people whom no one regarded.

Such are some of old Polly's memories as she puts down her pail and looks towards where the mill used to stand. Some of them are known to others through the casual boasts and later complaints of her husband at the 'Good Intent,' and now by her own wandering talk. Wilcocks was determined to enjoy his life as the husband of an heiress, and spent all her savings in keeping up his dignity before he took to his bed and died dissatisfied, but uncomplaining.

In the almshouses she leads a life of solitude, due to her own pride and the malice of her fellows, which keeps it alive. 'There's old Polly Wilcocks,' they say, 'who doesn't own the parish. There's Lady Muck upon Dung Hill.' Each new-comer she hopes to turn into a retainer to her family glories, and for a day or two she wins a certain respect for her dignity and ghostly claim, and then has to shut herself up alone with her scorn. She still calculates with augmented fantasy, but ever less and less skill, the sum of money which would now have been hers if she had had her right. She will stop one when she has been dipping her pail by the bridge and point to where the mill roof and chimneys used to stand out clear against a steep meadow behind, and she will say:

'By rights all that is mine,' and move her arm slowly, as if it were thinking, across a sunlit landscape. 'It was my father's and I was the only child. He wasn't hardly right in his mind and I have never had a penny, not a penny. There's Golden Rose farm and Crossways and New House and Knobsworth. . . . They are mine and I don't want to tell my business, but I know what they are worth, of course I do. They had no right to pull down the mill: they never asked me. And what did they find in the chimney? Aha! but there's one thing the fools have never done,' and she whispers to herself, 'they have never drained the pond.' One day she stood watching the sloping fields and the sheep which the late August sun turned into gold, every one into distinct soft, warm gold. 'Not a blade of grass has any right to grow there now,' she mused, 'because they who take the rent are not the owners. Not an ear of corn, not a mangold, not so much as a honeysuckle on the hedge that does nobody any good, ought to grow without my leave. There is no justice in the laws. Even God has forgotten me. I have cursed these fields in the night-time in that awful house where I live with those women, but it makes no difference. Look at those children in the brook. What business have they got to be there? I could forbid them if I liked, but they would take no notice, ignorant as they are.' She picks up her pail or without gratitude someone picks it up for her, and she turns her back on her fields and moves away slowly, stopping every hundred yards and looking back with bitterness, thinking of her great possessions. Yet they say she is not unhappy, that no one is likely to keep her room longer at the almshouse. When she steps inside her room and slams the door and once more her ear recognizes the sound of the mill water she has nothing pleasant or happy to remember, nothing that has been wasted, nothing she would have back again: she regrets only that her mother had been so weak as not to force Old Pile to marry her first and afterwards to make a sensible will, and for that she herself was not to blame.

For the whole of one year, whenever my daily walks led me down a certain old lane that used to be full of sun and forgetfulness, I was sure not to have it to myself. It was no longer used as a road, the farm it had served once being covered up in ivy and nettle; and as a footpath it was not a short cut to anywhere. Until that year I had met no one there. I have not met anyone there since. He was nearly always in the same place, just where the first bend in the lane shut out the road. At first, I thought he looked unusually out of place, with his new, stiff clothes, tall grey hat, polished ebony walking-stick, and movements angular and precise. I was not glad to see him – an invalid, I supposed – in a place which I once believed to be my own, and could not regard as a thoroughfare.

One day he stopped me by asking the name of a flower which he pointed out tenderly and politely with his glossy stick. As he spoke he turned his eyes towards me, though hardly upon me, so that I seemed to be bathed in their light, which had a cold brightness and purity as of newly melted frost, and a blissfulness also which was so intense as to be unearthly. Clearly he was one who saw invisible things. Feeling that he was not looking at me I could observe his eyes closely, and they

205

were indifferent to my curiosity. They were moistly bright, of a clear grey, and almost circular, the lids being unnoticeable under the gentle arches of thick, light-brown eyebrows; their expression was of childlike earnestness and simplicity, tinged with surprise that might almost have been fear. His face was square, and the delicate skin, drawn tightly over prominent bones, was nearly all concealed by the short brown hair on cheeks, lips, and chin. Through the hair showed a pair of lips matching the eyes – full, moist, shapely, and soft, of an unblemished innocence. He was short, squarely but lightly made. His voice was in keeping with eyes and lips; it was deep, slow, and soft almost to a breaking point.

I saw him many times before we spoke more than a few words again. As I passed he used to cast upon me that bright, unchanging glance without any kindliness in its gentleness, and seemed to feel rather than to see that I was on that common plane where everybody knows what you mean because you mean nothing in particular. In reply I could only look upon him with curiosity that was quickly overcome by discomfort, by awe, and even a kind of dread. Beauty, genius, or happiness, each in its own way, compels awe akin to fear, in the detached beholder. This man had happiness. Never before or since have I seen happiness so shining. Where at first I had blindly seen only his external incongruity with the untended hawthorns and virgin grass, I came to see perfect fitness. He was entirely at home there. In my memory the intensity of his happiness is all the more wondrous because of the pain of his end not much more than a year after I saw him first.

He knew himself that he was to die soon.

He was the son of a farmer among the mountains. When he had to go to school at eight or nine years old, it was in a town within sight of the ridges, but thirty miles away. In the town he had grown up. He was there when his father died, and except on the day of the funeral he never revisited his home. Tired of school, he left of his own accord and became a collier. For six days out of seven he washed only his lips clean, and that with ale. At the end of the sixth he washed the whole of his face, that he might kiss a maid. He fell in love. But the maid died, and at her funeral he dropped, fainting, into the grave. From that day he began to read all night. He seldom saw the sun, except on Sundays, and then only through the windows of his bedroom where he worked, or of his chapel. He began to preach, and in a few years was thought fit to be a minister. His furious pieties in the pulpit won him at first a congregation that would travel many mountain leagues on horseback or on foot to hear him. But out of the pulpit he was a different man. He was silent and morose. He would take no part in festivals, in music, in politics, in judgments of erring man or woman. They thought him proud; they muttered that they would not go on paying a man to mount up into the clouds for one day in the week, and when he had recovered from a long illness, he found he must go to a small house in the hills to serve two chapels many miles apart. He had loved God overmuch. But he did not cease from loving. God hid Himself from this worshipper, but he kneeled and smiled as if God had loved him. He thought of no one else; there was none but Him and of Him he thought as winter changed to spring, and spring to summer, and summer to winter, as roads glide into one another. He did not look down to behold the earth and sea, nor up to the sky. There was nothing for him but God, and the two little grey chapels far from man, on the great moors.

Once again he fell ill and in his delirium the truth passed before his eyes – that he had loved God overmuch and His creatures too little. Sickness left him unable to walk any more from chapel to chapel over the cloudy hills. He had to teach little children in a hamlet so poor that they were glad of him. There he lived alone, except for the children and the birds that inhabit the lean oaks of the stony copses, the alders along the brooks, the fern upon the lone crag that filled half of his northern sky. Since his illness he had forgotten about God, and remembered only the misery of his creatures. But the children and the birds cheered and taught him. On this earth he learned that it was a man's part to love the earth and its children. There would be plenty of time left in eternity for loving God. We do not demand, he reflected, that the maidservant lighting a fire at dawn should think about the sun, or that the soldier loading his rifle should think about his king; and so an earthly man need not greatly be troubled about anything but his fellow-men and animals, companions of the brief lifetime that is as a meadow in one of the folds of the mountain of eternity. In those old days, he thought, when the Lord went over Jordan with the children of Israel, men were as children, and He walked with them, but now He has ascended and we see Him not until we also shall have gone up, we know not whither. Nor did his thought perish when another sickness overthrew

him and left him one hand trembling as if it were
no longer his own. The children presented him
with the ebony stick, and he left them to die. In
the meantime he had taken to this lane.

Sometimes he brought a book out with him, and
when he did, it was a book of travel or natural
history. He had an inexhaustible desire to know
about everything that lives on the earth, both near
and far. He had learned the songs of many birds,
and spoke of them familiarly with admiration and
delight. The immensity and variety of Nature, as
he found himself, or read of it in the gorgeous
records of travellers, were a source of continual
satisfaction; he had never dreamed of them before.
Everywhere he found beauty, personality, and
differences without end. The old simplicity and
horror of the world conceived as the abode of evil
man and a dissatisfied, incompatible Deity were
forgotten. He could speak of God without
emotion. After reading a book in which a liberal
and gentle soul created a liberal and gentle Deity,
and showed the necessity for his own adherence
to the religion of his fathers, his only comment
was: 'It is a good book . . . a good God, but not
a very great God after all . . . What does that
thrush say? We must consider him. But so far
they do not seem to know very much about him,

except his skeleton and his diet. There must be one God for both of us. We can afford to wait. So can He.' But that was only a casual, light-hearted expression of the creed that was coming to him under the sky. He turned away to look at a blackcap singing every minute high up in golden-green blossom against the blue sky, where the sun and the south-west wind ruled over large, eager grey clouds with edges of gleaming white. The little dead-leaf coloured bird quivered all over; his throat swelled in bubble after bubble; his lifted black head was turned from side to side as he sang; and he moved slowly among the blossom.

The high, quick, dewy notes filled the paralytic with a thin, exquisite pleasure, as if his soul had climbed upon the line of his vision and crept into the singing bird. 'All these things are mine. They are me. And that is not all: I am them. We are one. We are organs and instruments of one an-other.' He did not forget the trees – 'those tethered dreamers, standing on one leg like Indian mystics.' With them also he felt the same com-munity, as though more rarely and in a way not to be spoken except by putting out his hand to touch their bark and leaves. The animals, too, were more remote than the birds, and reminded him too often of men's careless sins of cruelty. He did not preach kindness to animals, but pitied those men who had not yet awakened to the need of kindness, as if they must be suffering for the lack as much as the animals. He could not tell why men kept birds in cages to sing. Their freedom in living and dying was lovely to him. Every creature, including man, is best in freedom, he said, looking up at the white clouds coursing in the freedom that was from everlasting to everlasting. He sighed with regret, mingled with apology, as animals slipped away out of sight. Then he was glad to hear the blackbird and thrush again, the sweet, lively talking of the thrush and the pure melody of the blackbird. They were his favourites. He could talk of the different blackbirds he had known, and their places in town or wild, and describe their differences. With a little laugh, because he remembered the days before he had such thoughts, he said plainly that they had souls and lived, as we do, after death, though he did not know, nor perhaps did they, what life it might be. Only, there was one thing in the blackbird that he could not enjoy – probably, he admitted, because he could not understand; and that was the laughing, discordant notes that often concluded his song, especially in the late spring. This distressed him, partly because it was not musically in keeping with the song, and partly because the bird seemed to be laughing at himself. He had been reading Byron, and it reminded him of the way the poet sometimes wound up a stanza with a cynic phrase; and he could not enjoy this in bird or poet. Those birds were children of the sun, he said to himself. Before, if not above, all birds and all creatures, he loved the sun. The only time when he mentioned again the little grey chapel that stood highest among the mountains was to conjecture that it was built near the site of a temple for sun-worship. There were large upright stones in an adjoining field that were said to have formed part of a sun temple; and he liked to remember that. It was the God, not of the old stones, but of the chapel, that descended upon him in his last illness.

For weeks he lay sick and wild with dreams of the night and fears of the day. He raged and accused himself of unpardonable heresies, and defiance alternated with remorse. He was placid only while he whistled over and over again with unearthly sweetness and clearness, a fragment of one of the mountain songs of the blackbird, heard far away in the wild lands. It was a fantastic whim, for Whatever overpowered him in that friendless

213

death-chamber, amid snow and silence, to wrest such blasting discords out of an instrument that had seemed in the lane to know only natural joy and tranquillity. 'The little God,' he said, in one of his latest moments of relief, 'the little God torments me.' And again: 'But I go to the Great One. It is well.'

Friend of the blackbird, is it well?

IT was a part of the country I had never known before, and I had no connections with it. Once only, during infancy, I had stayed here at a vicarage, and though I have been told things about it which it gives me, almost as if they were memories, a certain pleasure to recall, no genuine memory survives from the visit. All I can say is that the name, Hereford, had somehow won in my mind a very distinct meaning; it stood out among county names as the most delicately rustic of them all, with a touch of nobility given it long ago, I think, by Shakespeare's 'Harry of Hereford, Lancaster, and Derby.' But now I was here for the third time since the year began. In April here I had heard, among apple trees in flower, not the first cuckoo, but the first abundance of day-long-calling cuckoos; here, the first nightingale's song, though too far-off and intermittently, twitched away by gusty night winds; here I found the earliest may-blossom which by May Day, while I still lingered, began to dapple the hedges thickly, and no rain fell, yet the land was sweet. Here I had the consummation of Midsummer, the weather radiant and fresh, yet hot and rainless, the white and the pink wild roses, the growing bracken, the last and best of the songs, blackbird's, blackcap's. Now it was August, and again no rain fell for many days; the harvest was a good one, and after standing long in the sun it was gathered in and put up in ricks in the sun, to the contentment of men and rooks. All day the rooks in the wheat-fields were cawing a deep sweet caw, in alternating choirs or all together, almost like sheep bleating, contentedly, on until late evening. The sun shone, always warm, from skies sometimes cloudless, sometimes inscribed with a fine white scatter miles high, sometimes displaying the full pomp of white moving mountains, sometimes almost entirely shrouded in dull sulphurous threats, but vain ones.

Three meadows away lived a friend, and once or twice or three times a day I used to cross the meadows, the gate, and the two stiles. The first was a concave meadow, in April strewn with daffodils. There, day and night, pastured a bay colt and a black mare, thirty years old, but gay enough to have slipped away two years back and got herself made the mother of this 'stolen' foal. The path led across the middle of the meadow, through a gate, and alongside one of the hedges of the next, which sloped down rather steeply to the remnant of a brook, and was grazed by half a dozen cows. At the bottom a hedge followed the line of the brook and a stile took me through it, with a deep drop, to a plank and a puddle, and so to the last field, a rough one. This rose up as steeply and was the night's lodging of four cart horses. The path, having gradually approached a hedge on the left, went alongside it, under the horse-chestnut tree leaning out of it, and in sight of the house, until it reached the far hedge and the road. There, at another stile, the path ceased. The little house of whitened bricks and black timbers lay a few yards up the road, a vegetable garden in front with a weeping ash and a bay-tree, a walnut in a yard of cobbles and grass behind, a yew on the roadside, an orchard on the other.

How easy it was to spend a morning or afternoon in walking over to this house, stopping to talk to whoever was about for a few minutes, and then strolling with my friend, nearly regardless of footpaths, in a long loop, so as to end either at his house or my lodging. It was mostly orchard and grass, gently up and down, seldom steep for more than a few yards. Some of the meadows had a group or a line of elms; one an ash rising out of an islet of dense brambles; many had several great old apple or pear trees. The pears were small brown perry pears, as thick as haws, the apples chiefly cider apples, innumerable, rosy and uneatable, though once or twice we did pick up a wasp's

217

remnant, with slightly greasy skin of palest yellow, that tasted delicious. There was one brook to cross, shallow and leaden, with high hollow bare banks. More than one meadow was trenched, apparently by a dried watercourse, showing flags, rushes, and a train of willows.

If talk dwindled in the traversing of a big field, the pause at gate or stile braced it again. Often we prolonged the pause, whether we actually sat or not, and we talked – of flowers, childhood, Shakespeare, women, England, the war – or we looked at a far horizon, which some dip or gap occasionally disclosed. Again and again we saw, instead of solid things, dark or bright, never more than half a mile off, the complete broad dome of a high hill six miles distant, a beautiful hill itself, but especially seen thus, always unexpectedly, through gaps in this narrow country, as through a window. Moreover, we knew that from the summit, between the few old Scots firs and the young ones of the plantation, we could command the Severn and the Cotswolds on the one hand, and on the other the Wye, the Forest of Dean, the island hills of North Monmouthshire, dark and massive, the remote Black Mountains pale and cloud-like, far beyond them in Wales. Not that we often needed to escape from this narrow country, or that, if we

did, we had to look so far. For example, the cloud
and haze of a hot day would change all. As we sat
on a gate, the elms in a near hedge grew sombre,
though clear. Past them rose a field like a low
pitched roof dotted over with black stooks of beans
and the elms at the top of that rise looked black
and ponderous. Those in farther hedges were
dimmer and less heavy, some were as puffs of
smoke, while just below the long straight ridge of
the horizon, a mile or two away, the trees were no
more than the shadows of smoke.

Lombardy poplars rose out from among the
elms, near and far, in twos and threes, in longer or
shorter lines, and at one point grouping themselves like the pinnacles of a cathedral. Most
farm-houses in the neighbourhood, and even pairs
of cottages, possessed a couple or more. If we got
astray we could steer by this or that high-perched
cluster, in which, perhaps, one tree having lost a
branch now on one side, now on the other, re-
sembled a grass stalk with flowers alternating up it.
When night came on, any farm-house group might
be transmuted out of all knowledge, partly with
the aid of its Lombardy poplars. There was also
one tree without a house which looked magnificent
at that hour. It stood alone, except for a much
lesser tree, as it were, kneeling at its feet, on the

long swooping curve of a great meadow against the sky; and when the curve and the two trees upon it were clear black under a pale sky and the first stars, they made a kind of naturally melodramatic 'C'est l'empereur' scene, such as must be as common as painters in a cypress country.

Whatever road or lane we took, once in every quarter of a mile we came to a farm-house. Only there by the two trees we tasted austere inhuman solitude as a luxury. Yet a man had planted the trees fifty or sixty years back. (Who was it, I wonder, set the fashion or distributed the seedlings?) It was really not less human a scene than that other one I liked at nightfall. Wildly dark clouds broke through the pallid sky above the elms, shadowy elms towering up ten times their diurnal height; and under the trees stood a thatched cottage, sending up a thin blue smoke against the foliage, and casting a faint light out from one square window and open door. It was cheerful and mysterious too. No man of any nation accustomed to houses but must have longed for his home at the sight, or have suffered for lacking one, or have dreamed that this was it.

Then one evening the new moon made a difference. It was the end of a wet day; at least, it had begun wet, had turned warm and muggy, and at last fine but still cloudy. The sky was banded with rough masses in the north-west, but the moon, a stout orange crescent, hung free of cloud near the horizon. At one stroke, I thought, like many other people, what things that same new moon sees eastward about the Meuse in France. Of those who could see it there, not blinded by smoke, pain, or excitement, how many saw it and heeded? I was deluged, in a second stroke, by another thought, or something that overpowered thought. All I can tell is, it seemed to me that either I had never loved England, or I had loved it foolishly, æsthetically, like a slave, not having realized that it was not mine unless I were willing and prepared to die rather than leave it as Belgian women and old men and children had left their country. Something I had omitted. Something, I felt, had to be done before I could look again composedly at English landscape, at the elms and poplars about the houses, at the purple-headed wood-betony with two pairs of dark leaves on a stiff stem, who stood sentinel among the grasses or bracken by hedge-side or wood's-edge. What he stood sentinel for I did not know, any more than what I had got to do.